The Grammar Answer KEY

Short Explanations to 100 ESL Questions

Keith S. Folse

University of Michigan Press
Ann Arbor

ISBN-13: 978-0-472-03718-6 (paper)
ISBN-13: 978-0-472-12381-0 (ebook)

2021   2020   2019   2018   4   3   2

◆◆◆ CONTENTS

◆◆◆ INTRODUCTION

Like most new teachers, I was extremely nervous when I first started teaching. In fact, in my first few years of teaching, I used to plan each of my ESL classes in excessive detail. Planning as much of the class as possible meant that there was less chance for something to go wrong, and if nothing could go wrong, then I did not need to be so nervous.

No matter how much I planned, however, students would sometimes ask me the most unanticipated questions. In my early years, I did not know how to answer many of these unexpected questions. Standing there at the board with an I-have-no-idea look on my face caused me a great deal of distress. As an eager new educator, I really wished I could handle these questions better. Sadly, I believed I was losing credibility with my students because I was a very young teacher who found himself saying "I don't know" far too often.

In teaching a lesson one day on *was* and *were*, I wrote this example sentence on the board: *George Washington* _____ *born on February 22, 1732.* My goal for this class was to get the students to talk about why we use *was* here instead of *were*, and I also wanted them to verbalize why *was* is a better choice than *is*.

I thought the lesson was very successful. The students talked about why *was* is better than *were*, and they discussed why *was* is better than *is*. My students really seemed to understand the material. To close the lesson, I then did what all good teachers do. I asked the class if they had any questions. Sure enough, a hand went up. I was of course anticipating a question about *was* or *were*. If not that, then maybe it would be a question about the pronunciation of *Washington*. But, those were not topics for this student's question that day.

"Teacher," the student began. "Why do you say *on February*? I thought *in February* is correct."

Imagine my surprise. I was anticipating a *was-were* question based on the lesson, not one about prepositions. I knew how to answer a question about *was* because I had planned that lesson in great detail, but I most definitely did not know why we use *in* instead of *on*. I tried to come up with some sort of explanation on the spot, but I really didn't know the reason why we use *in* or *on* with certain time words. (See Questions 35 and 36 in this book for the explanation.)

To be certain, it is OK for a teacher not to know the answer to every student question, and it is OK to say to a student, "I don't know the answer to that question, but I'll find out and let you know tomorrow." However, to maintain your credibility with students, it is <u>not</u> OK to say "I don't know" very often, and it is <u>not</u> OK to say "I don't know" when the questions are about basic ESL issues such as verb tenses (Questions 66, 67, 71, 72), the difference between *a* and *the* (Question 7), and the three ways we pronounce *–ed* (Questions 48, 49, 50). As a trained professional, you need to know these basic ESL grammar issues.

In my first few years of teaching, I tried hard to handle these unexpected grammar questions better. To reach this goal, my strategy was to arrive at school extra early to talk to the much more experienced teachers in the teachers' lounge. Those teachers seemed to know everything.

I would ask, "Why does my book have a chapter called *if*?" or "Why don't we say **homeworks* or **informations*?" or "The affirmative is *I went*, so why isn't the negative **I didn't went*?" I don't think I ever asked a question that someone in that room could not answer immediately. I was—and remain years later—envious and in awe of the amazing information my colleagues had in their heads and could explain to me in detail, seemingly without much effort. They were the ESL teachers that I wanted to be.

At a K–12 teacher conference some two decades later, I was doing a workshop on recognizing and explaining ESL errors. The last error we discussed that day was why ESL learners tend to pronounce every *–ed* past tense ending as a separate syllable, such as **miss-ed* for *missed* and **clean-ed for cleaned*. After the workshop, a teacher approached me and said, "You know, I've heard my students say these errors, and now I understand why they do this. Is this kind of information written down anywhere?"

That teacher's comment was the catalyst that inspired me to write *Keys to Teaching Grammar to English Language Learners* and this book of ESL student questions about grammar. I've written

---

NOTE: In ESL grammar and linguistics books, an asterisk (*) is placed before examples that are not grammatical in English and typically not made by native speakers.

these books for teachers who, like me many years ago, want to know as much about English as a second language as they possibly can so they will be able to help their students more.

To remedy this situation, I have collected questions from ESL teachers all over the world. In this book, I offer the answers to some of the more common questions that are hard to answer. While this information may seem overwhelming in terms of volume, I assure you there is some very good news: The same questions tend to come up in class over and over. After you've taught for just a few years, you will even come to know that a Spanish speaker will ask you about *be* vs. *have* (Question 83), a Chinese speaker may use *even though* and *but* in the same sentence (Question 25), and an Arabic speaker will overuse the definite article *the* (Question 8).

I wish I had had this kind of resource when I was first teaching. Perhaps I wouldn't have been so nervous in those early years and therefore would have been a more effective teacher earlier in my career.

After reading the material in this book, you will start to recognize your learners' errors much more easily. I hope you find this book useful. As you read the 100 questions and answers, you may wish for more information or you may have other questions that should appear in a future book. In those cases, please write me at mygrammarquestion@gmail.com. I look forward to hearing from you.

Organization of This Book

This book is a collection of 100 questions submitted by ESL teachers—both novice and experienced as well as native speakers and non-native speakers—from many different countries around the world. The questions are real questions students have asked about English.

The questions have been organized into 12 chapters on topics that teachers and students can relate to very well: *Adjectives, Articles, Clauses, Connectors, Gerunds and Infinitives, Prepositions, Pronouns, Pronunciation, Subject-Verb Agreement, Suffixes, Verbs,* and *Vocabulary Meets Grammar.* The number of questions in each chapter ranges from 3 to 18 and is based on the types of questions that teachers submitted.

Each chapter begins with a short overview of the chapter's topic. Sometimes key grammar terminology tied to that area of grammar is introduced. Each overview ends with a chart explaining three common errors commonly made by English learners attempting to use that grammatical feature.

For each of the 100 questions, the question is presented in a box. An answer then follows that contains information that could inform teachers' instruction. The answer often contains charts that depict the grammar patterns more clearly. If a grammar item tends to be problematic for certain language groups, that connection is also mentioned.

To make it easier to locate information that teachers need about students' English language difficulties, this book also includes: a review of the parts of speech, a glossary of important grammar terminology (glossed terms are boldfaced in the text), and a detailed index (by question number, not page number). For example, if a student asks whether to say *I am boring* or *I am bored*, you may not know that that is a question about adjectives, but you could look in the index and find this topic referenced by entries for *–ing/–ed*, adjectives, and past participle.

Audience

The contents of this book are valuable to a variety of teachers:

- K–12 teachers: Whether you are a 2nd grade science teacher or a 9th grade history teacher, this book will help you become familiar with ESL errors. It will also help you understand why they are made and how you could offer corrections.
- Grammar teachers: If you teach a grammar course in an intensive English program or a college course, this book will help you gain extra information about some of the types of questions your students are likely to ask you in class. You might recognize the titles of the 12 chapters in this book as also being part of the table of contents of whatever grammar textbook you are using in your grammar course.
- Writing instructors: If you teach composition at the high school or college level, the information in many of these questions will help you understand why your ESL writers make certain errors in their writing. In particular, frequent errors with articles, clauses, connectors, gerunds and infinitives, suffixes, or verbs can skew a reader's perception of the quality of an ESL student's written work, so writing instructors need to recognize these as typical ESL errors and consider ways to help their ESL writers reduce them.

◆ Adult ESL teachers: Adult ESL learners are working hard to improve their overall English proficiency. Because many of them take only a few hours of classes per week, one objective of these classes is to help these learners recognize the gap between correct English production and their own emergent English. For example, an adult who says *in Monday* when conversing with native-speaking work colleagues will receive no correction because native speakers who are interested in having a conversation do not usually correct that person's English mistakes. In fact, in this example of *in Monday*, a native speaker would probably understand what was meant and not even notice the error. Teachers of adult ESL classes need to be aware of what some of their students' most common errors are so they can help them improve their English.

◆ English as a Foreign Language (EFL) teachers: In many EFL settings around the world, English-speaking teachers with little to no English language training are hired to teach English conversation. Sometimes new EFL conversation teachers think they do not need to know about ESL grammar because the class is conversation, but they quickly find that their learners make a lot of errors that need teacher intervention. Students will want to know why the lesson about a recipe for making cookies used *how many* for *cups* but *how much* for *flour* (Question 85). The questions and answers in this book can help these teachers understand their learners' difficulties in English more quickly and be prepared to provide explanations, as well as teach ESL lessons better.

This book can also be a valuable resource in a variety of different situations:

1. in-service professional development (P.D.) workshops for any type of teacher training, ranging from intensive English programs to K–12 districts
2. an EFL conversation teacher—native or non-native speaker —who may not be fully aware of the structures used in English as a foreign language
3. training for college or university writing center tutors who interact with non-native writers' papers
4. any education course that trains future K–12 teachers

5. a TEFL course (undergraduate or graduate)
6. a Methods course in a TESOL program
7. a Practicum course
8. a grammar or structure course in a TESOL program
9. a course on second language writing
10. a course on second language speaking

The Questions Our English Language Learners Have about English

Many of the questions that our students ask us are the result of differences between how English expresses an idea and how another native language expresses the same idea. This native language interference can cause problems. In English, you *are hungry,* but in Spanish, you *have hunger* (Question 83). In English, I am married *to* Susan, but in French, I am married *with* Susan (Question 37). In English, *I have flown* an airplane, but in Japanese, *as for me, there is experience of flying airplane* (Question 72). In English, *Mr. Smith is a* teacher; in Arabic, *the Mr. Smith* teacher (Question 6, 7, 83).

It is very common for language learners to make mistakes when they translate something word for word. The result is that you have interference from the first language because the two languages are different.

How much of one language is similar to the new language? How much is different? The differences are important for all learners to consider when they are learning a new language. In fact, it is often these differences that account for the questions that our students ask us in class.

To help you learn more about these **interference** errors, you should begin making a list. If you are familiar with the English of ESL students, perhaps you can make a list of 10 to 20 errors frequently made by speakers of a certain language. In addition, conducting an internet search of "common English errors made by _____ speakers" (fill in the blank with a native language such as Spanish, Korean, or Japanese) will help you locate a list. Use the list to help increase understanding of why the student is making the error. Give students a copy of the list and ask them to study the most frequent of these errors one by one. The first step for learners to reduce errors is to recognize that they make those errors.

Two useful resources for learning about typical errors made by speakers of a certain language are the 16 Native Language Interference charts in *Keys to Teaching Grammar to English Language Learners, 2nd Edition* (Folse, 2016), as well as *Learner English* (Swan & Smith, 2001).

This chart shows some common errors made by speakers of different languages (but not just the language listed) that are caused by interference from translating.

Native Language	Learner Error from Native Language Interference	Correct English Sentence
Arabic	*The honesty is important.	Honesty is important.
	*This is the pen I bought it yesterday.	This is the pen I bought yesterday.
Chinese	My sister is a doctor. *He is 42.	My sister is a doctor. She is 42.
	*Even though it's late, but I'm not sleepy.	Even though it's late, I'm not sleepy.
French	That's not John's car. *Her car is red.	That's not John's car. His car is red.
	*Mary speaks very well English.	Mary speaks English very well.
Japanese	*I have stayed in Tokyo from 2014 to 2016.	I stayed in Tokyo from 2014 to 2016.
	*I read book in school.	I read books in school.
Korean	*I didn't like the game. I was boring.	I didn't like the game. I was bored.
	*I went to home late.	I went home late.
Portuguese	*She has 19 years.	She is 19 years old.
	*The people is in favor of this new plan.	The people are in favor of this new plan.
Russian	*He is good teacher.	He is a good teacher.
	*I am agree with you.	I agree with you.
Spanish	*I have hungry.	I am hungry.
	*They bought a car white.	They bought a white car.
Vietnamese	*My brother live there.	My brother lives there.
	*My pet is cat.	My pet is a cat.

What Do We Mean by "Correct" English Grammar?

Some languages have an official group of people who decide what is and is not correct usage. The French language, for example, has the French Academy, which was founded in 1635. The 40 members are called immortals, and new members are chosen by the existing members. The French Academy is the official authority on the French language. As such, it publishes an official dictionary of French. Likewise, the Royal Spanish Academy, founded in 1713, has a similar function with the Spanish language. The Royal Spanish Academy works with organizations in 22 other Spanish-speaking countries. Other languages that have similar official organizations include Arabic, Cantonese, Czech, Dutch, Italian, Nepali, Persian, and Russian.

English, however, does not have such an organization. Instead, correct usage in English has been determined over the years by a range of people, from religious leaders to eminent scholars, dictionary writers, and TV broadcasters. The bottom line is that no single person or organization or even country now dictates what is and is not correct English, which explains why people are often unclear about the status of a certain language usage in English.

There are two different approaches to determining what correct language usage is. When analyzing a given sentence, the traditional prescriptive approach tells us what is correct and what is wrong. In contrast, a descriptive approach would consider who produced the sentence and under what conditions—that is, was it written or spoken, for example? How old was the person? Was the speaker a man or a woman? What was the relationship between the speaker (or writer) and the audience? For example, in a prescriptive approach, *whom* would be required in the question *Whom did you call?* However, a descriptive approach would recognize that, today, almost everyone would almost universally ask, *Who did you call?* In a descriptive approach, *whom* is grammatically accurate, but it is more likely used by older speakers than younger speakers and in very formal settings and almost never in everyday conversation.

To answer the question of "What is correct English usage?" it is very important for us to remember that this book is aimed at teachers of non-native speakers who are learning English. First and foremost, teachers should teach what students need. If your students only want to improve their conversation, then you should teach students about forms that are common in conversation. On the other hand, if your students need to write academic papers, then you should teach grammatical patterns that are favored in academic writing. Therefore, students writing an academic paper should write *The patient <u>for whom</u> the doctor had written the prescription died*, but they should be taught that speaking this way could certainly draw negative attention. In normal conversation, learners should say *The patient <u>who</u> the doctor had written the prescription <u>for</u> died*.

Students who are attempting a new language do not want to be bombarded with a lot of extra information. Therefore, teachers should exercise caution with how much information is taught when any new language form is introduced. The standard form should be taught, and once students are comfortable with this new form, then the teacher can and should address any variations that students may encounter from native speakers or may themselves use when speaking with people in their own age or social group.

For example, a grammar point that ESL students learn at the beginning level is the conjugation of verbs in the simple present tense: *I need, you need, he needs, she needs, it needs, we need, they need*. The difficult part is the addition of *–s* for *he, she,* and *it*. The negative form is *does not* or *doesn't*, such as *she doesn't need*. However, learners who listen to songs will almost never hear the word *doesn't*. Instead, they will hear a non-standard form of *he/she/it don't,* as in these song titles: *He Don't Love You (Like I Love You)* and *It Don't Matter to Me*. In addition, learners may be interacting with native speakers who routinely use *he/she/it don't*.

The message here for teachers is twofold. The first part involves what should be taught and when it should be taught. If a grammar point has a standard usage and a frequent non-standard usage, teachers should first teach the standard form and allow learners to become familiar with that form. If—and this is a huge caveat—teachers really think that students would benefit from knowing the non-standard form as well, then they should introduce that non-standard form and clearly explain any limitations, such as who typically uses this form, when they might use it, and very importantly, how ESL students will be perceived if they use this non-standard form. Will they sound cool? Will they sound young? Will they sound uneducated? Will they sound impolite? Teachers should be aware that some forms of English that once were non-standard but now seem ubiquitous have implied associations about status (class or level of education)—that is, something uttered by someone from one group may be evaluated as "cool" but that, when uttered by someone from another group, may be judged in a negative way.

The second part of the message here for all teachers is that you need to know the grammar of English inside out. You need to know the standard form, and you need to be aware of what the non-standard form is. You also need to have a good idea about what kind of person would use this non-standard form. You need to explain to college students that they may need to use one form to blend in with other college students but a different form in their general English or when in a high-stakes situation, like when applying for a job. Teachers cannot teach what they themselves do not know, so teachers need to learn extensively about English grammar. Teachers also need to know not to attempt to explain everything when a second language learner is attempting a new grammar structure.

Quiz: How Much ESL Grammar Do You Already Know?

Here is an opportunity for you to see how much you know about ESL errors. Each of these examples was written or said by an ESL learner. Can you find the one or two errors in each sentence, correct them, and then explain what the problem is? The language in parentheses indicates the language of the person who wrote or said this sentence, but each error may be typical of more than one language.

1. My family and I came to this country for begin a new life. (Spanish)

2. My sister and me love the jewelry. (Arabic)

3. In the future, I want study biology and become the most smart dentist in my country. (Spanish)

4. If I can speak English well, I can get good job later. (Chinese)

5. My friends went to the Disney World yesterday, but I have never gone to there. (Japanese)

6. My name is Ahmad, and I from the Kuwait City. (Arabic)

7. I like miso soup because it is really good taste. (Japanese)

8. Our teacher always give us a homework every day. (Korean)

9. I am from Turkey, but I have been in United States since 2016. (Turkish)

10. When I was a child young, I wanted to be a bus driver, but after awhile, I was no longer interesting in driving a bus. (Spanish)

11. My mother is teacher in elementary school. (Arabic)

12. If I improve my English, I can talking with my American friends. (Chinese)

13. I was married on August. (Arabic)

14. I was born in New York, but I live in Peru my whole life. (Turkish)

15. My hobbies are play the soccer and going to the gym. (Portuguese)

16. My name is Daniel, and I have sixteen years old. (Spanish)

17. In my country, I work for the traffic office, so I am interested in the traffic problems. (Chinese)

18. I always dream of go to many countries. (Vietnamese)

19. I like many things, but my favorite activities for fun is football and music. (French)

20. I love Italian food, but I like eat a lot different kinds of food. (Russian)

21. In this class, I hope have fun and learn a lot of English. (German)

22. As a teenager, I played only baseball but I also considered others sports like tennis and badminton. (Korean)

23. *Opening* and *begining* are two words that some people do not spell them correctly. (Arabic)

24. My sister love me very much and always gives me advices about life. (Vietnamese)

25. I love my country very much. Is awesome place to live. (Spanish)

26. Today my life is very good, but it is no easy to have a good life in my country. (Portuguese)

27. Last summer I have been in Malta for six weeks. (German)

28. I was born and grow up in Japan. (Japanese)

29. Last summer I could visit many country, and I liked them very much. (Spanish)

30. After I graduate from college, I want to become a English teacher one day. (Japanese)

Acknowledgments

No work is the result of just one person. This book was inspired by the many teachers who have attended my grammar and vocabulary workshops and the hundreds of students in my ESL and TESOL/TEFL courses over the years.

I would also like to thank two professors who invited me to visit, via Skype, their grammar courses for future teachers many times. For several years, Dr. Elizabeth O'Dowd (St. Michael's College, Vermont, USA) and Dr. Deborah Crusan (Wright State University, Ohio, USA) have allowed me to be a guest lecturer in their classes once each semester to field their students' questions about grammar. A good number of those questions were in fact selected for this book.

I am indebted to the three readers who gave me invaluable feedback on the questions and answers: Deborah Mitchell (Idaho, USA), Kim Hardiman (Florida, USA), and Mauricio Arango (Colombia). Each of the 100 questions was rewritten and sometimes rethought completely based on their insightful suggestions.

I am especially grateful to Kelly Sippell, my editor at the University of Michigan Press, who gave hours of her time and dozens of innovative ideas in helping this book come to fruition. Once again, with this project, she went above and beyond what was merely required. It is because of her dedication to the University of Michigan Press and her profession that this book is the solid work that it has become.

Finally, I am indebted to Dr. Melanie Gonzalez and Dr. Alison Youngblood for helping collect the questions as well as to the many teachers who submitted questions for this work from countries all over the world, including Brazil, Cameroon, Canada, China, Colombia, Ecuador, France, Greece, Guatemala, Iran, Iraq, Italy, Japan, Mexico, Panama, Peru, Poland, Russia, Saudi Arabia, Senegal, South Korea, Spain, Taiwan, Thailand, Turkey, United Arab Emirates, the U.S., Uzbekistan, and Venezuela. Hundreds of questions were collected over a ten-year period. For any contributors' names or locations I have inadvertently omitted or misidentified, I apologize in advance.

Some of the 100 questions used in this book were submitted by: Mohamad Abouda (Senegal), Mauricio Acosta (Colombia), Enid Akers (Orlando, Florida, USA), Salman Alabdadi (graduate student, California, USA), Mais Al-Jabbawi (Iraq), Uthman Alzuhairy (Saudi Arabia), Kenny Anderson (Florida, USA), Alla Askarova (Education

Complex, Baku, Azerbaijan), Jackie Avery (Turkey), Anne Bachmann (Clackamas Community College, Oregon, USA), Carol Bandar (Saddleback College, California, USA), Patricia Baptiste (College of New Jersey, USA), Robert Bennear (Utah, USA), Jill Blanc (Orlando, Florida, USA), Aneta Braczyk (New Jersey, USA), Paula Bramante (University of Minnesota, USA), Sibley Brown (Morocco), Kate Brummett (Florida, USA), Keisha Bryant (Tennessee State University, USA), Lisa Byrum (Baker Elementary School, Little Rock, Arkansas, USA), Jose Carrizo (Panama), Grace Cassagnol (U.S. Peace Corps, Senegal), Maria Castillo (Orlando, Florida, USA), Samantha Cawle (Saudi Arabia), Annie Cheung (graduate student, California State University, Fullerton, USA), Ya-Chen Chien (Taiwan), Karina Clemmons (University of Arkansas, USA), Mario Coello (California, USA), Miranda Creech (Panama), Deborah Crusan (Wright State University, Ohio, USA), Nikki Decoteau (New Hampshire, USA), Paul Delaunay (Centro de Idiomas, Chihuahua, Mexico), Alya Devydenko (Ukraine), Luciana Diniz (Portland Community College, Oregon, USA), Michelle Donate (Vietnam), Luciana Dugniolle (Orlando, Florida, USA), Andres Camilo Echeverri (Colombia), Bernice Ege-Zavala (School of Teaching ESL, Seattle, Washington, USA), Ruby Eichenour (Community College of Aurora, Colorado, USA), Eman Elturki (Washington State University, USA), Claudia Fernandez (Bilkent University, Turkey), Linda Fitzgibbon (Hankuk University of Foreign Studies, Seoul, South Korea), Amanda Fleming (English Teaching Assistant, Fulbright Program, Vietnam), Celeste Flowers (University of Central Arkansas, USA), Brandon Gay (Wright State University, Ohio, USA), Pompeya Gettler (K.O. Knudson Middle School, Las Vegas, Nevada, USA), Melanie Gonzalez (Salem State University, Massachusetts, USA), Lisa Gonzalves (graduate student, California, USA), Claudio Acevedo Gordillo (Argentina), Victor Gosse (Ghana), Jenny Graham (Cypress College, California, USA), Valerie Martin Grosso (Orlando, Florida, USA), Martin Guerra (Mountain View College, Dallas, Texas, USA), Brigitte Gueter (Windsor, Canada), Michael Hajj (ATEL, Lebanon), Cate Hall (Queensland University of Technology, Australia), Bethany Hallid (Maine, USA), Joe Hamilton (Seattle Pacific University, Washington, USA), Kim Hardiman (Orlando, Florida, USA), Daryl Hausman (LEAP Program, Wright State University, Ohio, USA), Shota Hayashi (Japan), Mary Helldorfer-Cooney (The Genesis Center, Rhode Island, USA), Shannon Herbert (Wright State University, Ohio, USA), Iliana

Higa (Chihuahua, Mexico), Jacque Hildreth (Skagit College ESL, Washington, USA), Giang Hoang (Evans Community Adult School, Los Angeles, California, USA), Farhad Hosseinabadi (Iran), Francesca Hulin (Yuba College, Marysville, California, USA), Julie Ingber (California, USA), Leah Jackson (Miami Dade College, Florida, USA), Cynthia Jankovic (Baghdad, Iraq), Lena Jensen (California, USA), Kathy Jiménez (Miami Dade College, Florida, USA), Wendy Jimenez (Instituto Guatemalteco Americano, Guatemala), Basil Keilani (South Korea), Kristina Kellerman (Cascadia College, Washington, USA), Amelie Kelly (Dongguk University, Gyeongju, South Korea), Meredith Kemper (University of Central Arkansas, USA), Koffi Kouadio (Ivory Coast), Megan Kropfelder (Wright State University, Ohio, USA), Rose Lake (Wright State University, Ohio, USA), Rebecca Lammons (University of Monterrey, Mexico), Chris Laning (Orlando, Florida, USA), Li Li (Vermont, USA), Ann Lippencott, University of California—Santa Barbara, USA), Joanne Locnikar (ABC Adult School, California, USA), Audra Lowery (Little Rock, Arkansas, USA), Maria Lumanatao (South Korea), Huiyuan "Tia" Luo (China), Sarah McGinley (Wright State University, Ohio, USA), Conor McGuire (Vermont, USA), Julien McNulty (South Korea), Myra Medina (Miami Dade College, Florida, USA), Mosebodi Metswamere (Vermont, USA), Shauna Mikulewicz (Taipei, Taiwan), Deborah Mitchell (Idaho, USA), Sheena Moleta (Florida, USA), Jonathan Murray (Mexico), Kristen Musser (Arkansas, USA), Ryan Nagel (China), Ndianko Ndao (Nigeria), Kimberley Neuterman (Madrid, Spain), Colin Nohr (Florida, USA), Meagan O'Connell (Valencia Community College, Florida, USA), Elizabeth O'Dowd (St. Michael's College, Vermont, USA), Dennis Oliver (Arizona, USA), Oriel Ortega (Panama City, Panama), Anthony Parlatti (Japan), Keith Petersen (Modesto Junior College, California, USA), Shroog Radain (Saudi Arabia), Susan Rainer (Arkansas, USA), Janet Raskin (Florida, USA), Noosha Ravaghi (San Diego, California, USA), Sara Reichel (English Teaching Assistant, Fulbright Program, South Korea), Andy Riner (Vermont, USA), Joshua Ripp (Shanghai, China), Bruce Rogers (independent consultant, Colorado, USA), Ryan Roling (School of Academic Advancement Madison Area Technical College, Wisconsin, USA), Henryjose Romero (Ecuador), Tom Rowe (Tulsa Community College, Oklahoma, USA), Wells Rutland (Afghanistan), Meredith Sagara (Dallas, Texas, USA), Lucy Sanford (Durham Continuing Education, Ontario, Canada), Christina Savvidis (Florida, USA),

Paul Schneider (Washington Academy of Languages, USA), Daniel Schweissing (Community College of Aurora, Colorado, USA), Monica Sebastiani (Italy), Amir Shafiee (Iran), Jeanne Sheehan (Santa Ana College, California, USA), Suzanne Sievert (Bellevue College, Washington, USA), Adelton Silva (Brazil), Susan Simpson (Maryland, USA), Larry Sims (Orange County, California, USA), Catarina Skiniotou (Greece), Alicia Slater (Vermont, USA), Olga Spraker (Broward College, Florida, USA), Karen Stanley (Central Piedmont Community College, North Carolina, USA), Gerry Stewart (Oviedo, Florida, USA), Brian Stoakley (South Korea), Lauren Swieter (Orlando, Florida, USA), Christopher Szczerba (English Teaching Assistant, Fulbright Program, Taiwan), Phillip Taylor (Tennessee, USA), Georgia Tate Troha (Japan), Heather Thompson (Bentonville High School, Arkansas, USA), Michelle Tygir (Japan), Laura Vance (Spring International Language Center, Arkansas, USA), Lisa Vorwerk (Danville Adult Learning Center, Arkansas, USA), Denise Whealan (Nevada Community College, USA), Justin Whittinghill (Japan), Aya Yamasaki (Japan), Alison Youngblood (Western Kentucky University, USA), Shiyao Yu (Japan), Xiaoli Yu (China), Kathleen Yun (Taiwan).

1 ◆ Adjectives

Adjectives are words that describe nouns or pronouns. They are an essential type of word in English and occur frequently, so students need to know how to use them correctly. For example, this simple sentence has three adjectives in it: *this, simple,* and *three*.

Everyone knows that there are **descriptive adjectives** such as *red, delicious, turbulent,* and *soft*, but there are other kinds of adjectives, too. **Possessive adjectives,** such as *my* car and *your* car, indicate whose car we are discussing. **Demonstrative adjectives** such as *this* and *that* also help the speaker and listener know which noun is being discussed. Numbers can also be adjectives: *one* idea, *six* ideas. **Articles** (*a, an, the*) can also be classified as adjectives because they describe a noun as specific or general. **Quantifiers,** such as *many* people, can also be adjectives. Grammatically there are many more types of adjectives than just descriptive adjectives.

3 Common ESL Errors with Adjectives

ESL Error	Explanation
1. *They have a house beautiful.	ESL students often place adjectives after nouns because this is how adjectives function in their native languages.
2. *These trees are very talls.	ESL students try to make adjectives plural because their native language requires adjectives to agree in number with a noun.
3. *I think Arabic is more difficult than English, and I think Spanish is more easy than English.	ESL students often use *more* to form the comparative form of all adjectives.

1

◆ **Question 1 Recognizing an Adjective**

How do you know if a word is an adjective?

Adjectives are words that describe nouns or pronouns. Common examples are *good, nice,* and *easy.*

There are several ways to recognize an adjective. One important way to recognize an adjective is by its location in the **phrase** or sentence, so word order is important. Adjectives generally occur in two different locations: (1) before a noun or (2) after the verb *be.*

Location	Examples
before a noun	*delicious* <u>soup</u>, *expensive* <u>shirts</u>, *green* <u>leaves</u>
after *be*	The soup <u>is</u> *delicious.* The shirts <u>were</u> *expensive.* The leaves <u>are</u> *green.*

We can also recognize an adjective by what it is doing in the sentence. Is it describing (*delicious*)? Is it identifying a specific noun (*the*)? Is it telling whether it is near (*this* book) or far (*that* book) from the speaker? Here are several categories of adjectives:

descriptive	*delicious, expensive, green*
articles	*a, an, the*
possessive	*my, your, her, their*
demonstrative	*this, that, these, those*
quantifier	*many, much, any*

We can also identify an adjective by the question it answers. Adjectives often tell **which one** (*This* book is mine), **how many** (I have <u>six</u> books), **how much** (No one received <u>any</u> mail today), or **what kind** (<u>Raw</u> milk can be dangerous).

Finally, another way to recognize some adjectives is by the ending (that is, the final suffix). According to the *Longman Grammar of Spoken and Written English* (Biber et al., 1999), the seven most frequent suffixes that mark an adjective are:

1. **–al** (*final, natural, social*)
2. **–ent** (*current, different, excellent*)
3. **–ive** (*active, passive, positive*)
4. **–ous/–ious** (*famous, obvious, serious*)
5. **–ate** (*accurate, private, separate*)
6. **–ful** (*beautiful, helpful, useful*)
7. **–less** (*endless, helpless, homeless*)

In addition, a useful and common adjective suffix is *–y* (*crazy, easy, funny, health, hilly, juicy, trendy, windy*).

However, many smaller adjectives do not have any overt endings: *cold, short, young.*

◆ Question 2 Order of Adjectives

What is the correct order of adjectives? Is it *a red book* or *a book red*? What happens if you have two adjectives? Is it *cotton white socks* or *white cotton socks*?

This is really two questions: (1) Do adjectives come before or after nouns? and (2) when there are two or more adjectives, what is the correct sequence?

A red book is correct. In English, adjectives come <u>before</u> nouns, which is also the case with Chinese, Japanese, Korean, Russian, German, and Bengali. In contrast, adjectives come <u>after</u> nouns in Spanish, Arabic, Vietnamese, Haitian Creole, French, Portuguese, Marshallese, and Italian. Therefore, Spanish speakers, for example, will often put adjectives after nouns in English, producing the error **a book red.*

White cotton socks is correct. The general rule is that adjectives come in this order: (1) opinion, (2) size, (3) age, (4) shape, (5) color, (6) origin, (7) material. *White* is a color and *cotton* is a material, so we have to put *white* before *cotton*. Many grammar books explain this rule, and students spend a lot of time memorizing the sequence and then completing many exercises. Although this information may certainly be useful for an English exam, it may not be so valuable for actually speaking English. The average native speaker tends to only use one or, occasionally, two adjectives to describe any given noun in everyday speech. Therefore, students who use more than two descriptive adjectives consecutively before a noun might sound odd.

This sequencing rule is also a good example of a grammar point that native speakers are never taught. It is not a problem for them since they acquired the correct order at an early age. This also means that if you ask native speakers who are not specially trained to teach English to non-native speakers why we say *white cotton socks* and not *cotton white socks*, they cannot answer the question. They usually say "It just sounds right," but that is not an explanation and not very helpful.

One final point here is that English also frequently uses nouns as adjectives. Examples include *a wool sweater, a bus station, a dinner invitation, a flower garden,* and *a wedding cake.* In academic or technical English, it is common to have multiple nouns functioning as adjectives. *A history test* is a test about history. *A history test question* is a question from a test about history. *A U.S. history test question* is a question from a test about the history of the U.S. When there is a true adjective and a noun functioning as an adjective, the true adjective goes first: *a new wool sweater,* not **a wool new sweater.* In general, the more adjective-like a word is, the farther to the left it goes. The more noun-like a word is, the farther to the right (or closer to the noun) it goes.

◆ **Question 3 Comparative and Superlative of Adjectives**

For comparison of adjectives, how do you know when to add
–er (*cheap → cheaper*) and when to use *more* (*expensive → more
expensive*)?

The **comparative** pattern here is fairly simple. In general, add –er
to one-syllable adjectives (*tall → taller*) and to one- and two-syllable
adjectives that end in –y: (*dry → drier, lazy → lazier*). All others use
more before: *expensive → more expensive*.

For the **superlative** form, the same rule applies for adding *the*
before the adjective and –est to the end of the adjective or using the
words *the most* before the adjective.

Adjectives with 1 Syllable			Adjectives with 1 or 2 Syllables, Ending in –*y*		
big	bigger	the biggest	busy	busier	the busiest
cheap	cheaper	the cheapest	silly	sillier	the silliest

Adjectives with 2 Syllables, Not Ending in –*y*	Adjectives with 3 or More Syllables
honest, more honest, the most honest	comfortable, more comfortable, the most comfortable
rapid, more rapid, the most rapid	difficult, more difficult, the most difficult

Past participles (which often end in –ed/–en) functioning as
adjectives are different. They use *more* for comparisons regardless
of the number of syllables that the adjective has. For example, *tired*
and *bored* have only one syllable, yet we say *more tired* and *more
bored*, not **tireder* and **boreder*.

There are a few one-syllable adjectives that do not use –er. Instead,
these adjectives use *more* in some cases: *more right, more fun*.

Some two-syllable adjectives, especially those stressed on the
first syllable, can also use –er: *more quiet* or *quieter, more simple* or
simpler.

There are few irregular forms: *good → better → the best; bad →
worse → the worst; far → farther/further → the farthest/the furthest*.

◆ **Question 4** *boring* vs. *bored* *(–ing* vs. *–ed* **adjectives)**

What's the difference between *boring* and *bored*? How do you know when to use an *–ing* adjective and when to use *–ed*?

In English, the suffixes *–ing* and *–ed* usually indicate verbs. However, we also have some pairs of adjectives where one form ends in *–ing* (*boring*) and the other form ends in *–ed* (*bored*). For English learners of many different first languages, these pairs can be very difficult to distinguish, especially in rapid conversation.

The *–ing* adjective form describes a person or thing that is causing a feeling, while the *–ed* adjective form describes how a person feels. For example, if you and I go to a movie and we do not like the movie, we might say *The movie is boring* because the movie is causing the feeling. However, we can also say *We are bored* because that is how we feel.

Other examples include:

- If you take a long trip, the trip is *tiring*, but you are *tired*.
- If you hear some big news, you are *surprised*, but the news is *surprising*.
- If you can't understand a question, the question is *confusing*, and you are *confused*.

A common mistake is when a student says **I am boring*. This sentence is theoretically possible, but it is an unlikely utterance. The correct sentence should be *I am bored*.

The *–ing* form is called the **present participle**, and the *–ed* form is called the **past participle**. However, one teaching suggestion is to avoid using these two labels and simply refer to them as the *–ing* adjective and the *–ed* adjective. A potential problem to be aware of when teaching is that some past participles end in *–en* (*written, rotten, spoken*).

◆ Question 5 Compound Adjectives

I found this sentence: "The couple has a ten-year-old child."
Why do you say *year* and not *years*? *Ten* is plural, so why not
ten years?

In this case, the phrase *ten-year-old* is an adjective describing
the noun *child*. All three words form one compound adjective. In
English, adjectives cannot be plural.

In *She is ten years old*, the phrase *ten years* is an adverb modifying
the adjective, so *years* is possible here.

Information	Compound Adjective
The car has four doors.	It is a four-door car.
The house has two stories.	It is a two-story house.
The exam had fifty questions.	It was a fifty-question exam.
The trip lasted three days.	It was a three-day trip.

Notice that the nouns after the numbers in the sentences in the
information column are plural (*doors, stories, questions, days*), but
the same nouns being used as adjectives in the second column are
not plural (*door, story, question, day*).

2 ◆ Articles

English has two types of articles: indefinite and definite. The **indefinite articles** include *a* and *an*. The **definite article** is *the*.

In ESL grammar, we also have a fourth option: **no article (null article)**. We often use no article when we refer to a whole category: *I like tennis*, not **I like the tennis*; *giraffes are interesting animals*, not **the giraffes are interesting animals*.

Native speakers do not see using no article as a separate option because they would never use an article in a sentence like **the cars use the gasoline*. However, many ESL students add *the* when they are referring to the whole category, such as **I like the sports* or **I do not like the spicy food*. When talking about the whole group and not a specific sport or a specific spicy food, we do not use any article.

3 Common ESL Errors with Articles

ESL Error	Explanation
1. *In my opinion, the giraffes are the most interesting animal on the planet.	ESL students often overuse *the* when they are referring to a whole category. Many times this is the result of translation from their native language.
2. *My brother has new bicycle.	In English, a singular count noun (*bicycle*) cannot exist without an article or similar word (*this*, *his*, *one*) in front of it. Many languages do not have a word for *a* or *an*, so this error is often the result of translation.
3. *I have a big homework tonight.	In English, non-count nouns like *homework* cannot be counted, so they cannot have a plural form. We cannot say **a homework* or **3 homeworks*.

♦ **Question 6** *a* vs. *an*

Do *a* and *an* have the same meaning? When do you use *a* and when do you use *an*?

A and *an* have the same meaning. They both mean "one."

The choice of *a* or *an* depends on the initial vowel sound of the next word. We use *an* when the next word begins with a vowel sound. It does not matter if the next word is a noun (*an answer*) or an adjective (*an excellent reason*).

Remember that the most important point here is the <u>sound, not the spelling.</u>

1. If the next word begins with a silent consonant letter but we say a vowel sound, use *an*:
   • *an hour, an honest person* (*h* is a consonant but is silent, so *hour* and *honest* begin with a vowel sound)
   • *a house, a heavy chair* (you hear *h*)
2. If the word begins with a vowel letter but we say a consonant sound, use *a*:
   • *a university, a unique experience, a European country* (*u* is a vowel but here it begins with the sound /y/, which is a consonant sound)
   • *an umbrella, an ugly fish* (you hear the **schwa** sound /ə/, which is a vowel sound).

◆ **Question 7 Indefinite Articles (*a, an*) and Definite Article (*the*)**

When do you use *a* and when do you use *the*?

There are two kinds of articles in English: **indefinite** and **definite**. **Indefinite articles** include *a* and *an*. They are called indefinite because they speak of any one thing in general that is not yet specified. The **definite article** is *the*, and it refers to something specific. Articles come before nouns (*a car, the bus*) or before an adjective in front of a noun (*a blue car, the best bus*).

Knowing how to use these articles correctly requires understanding nouns. In English, all nouns can be classified as count or noncount. **Count nouns** are nouns you can count, such as *1 cat, 2 cats* or *1 child, 2 children*; they can be singular or plural. A singular count noun has to have an article or other **determiner** in front of it. For example, the word *car* is a count noun, so in the singular, it needs *a, the, this, that, my, your, one,* etc., in front of it.

The **indefinite articles** *a/an* are used for singular count nouns. For speakers of languages that have no indefinite article (e.g., Arabic, Chinese, Japanese, Korean, Russian, Vietnamese), a common mistake is using a singular count noun with no article: **We have new car; *Bed is for sleeping; *My father is pilot.*

Non-count nouns are nouns that cannot be counted, such as *water, sand, homework, information,* and *advice.* For example, you cannot say **1 homework* or **2 homeworks.* If you cannot say **1 homework*, then you cannot say **a homework* because *1* and *a* have similar meanings.

Sometimes we can use *a* or *an* with a non-count noun, but the meaning changes. For example, in *I like chicken*, we are talking about something to eat, but in *I see a chicken*, we are talking about an animal. Sometimes using a non-count noun with *a* or *an* in a singular sense refers to containers or servings: we can say *I'll take a water*, but what we mean is a bottle of water.

Using *a / an*		
Usage	**Example**	**Meaning**
1. talking about a thing in general	I need a bicycle.	I don't care which bicycle I have.
2. something non-specific exists	There is a book on the table.	A non-specified book exists.
3. defining (singular)	Colombia is a country in South America.	We say what Colombia is. It is a country.
4. the first mention	Look! A rainbow is starting to form.	Prior to speaking, the rainbow was not mentioned.

Using *the*		
Usage	**Example**	**Meaning**
1. talking about a specific thing	The population of Mexico is about 130 million.	We are talking about the population of one specific country.
2. something known by both the speaker and the listener (or the writer and the reader)	Where is the market?	Both the speaker and the listener know which market is being discussed.
3. something unique, only one of	The moon was bright last night.	There is only one moon.
4. second mention	I bought a pair of shoes and some black socks yesterday. The socks are very comfortable.	Use *the* with socks because this is the second time we mention *socks*.
5. special cases (There are many special cases for the use of *the*.)	I like to play the guitar, but I don't enjoy playing basketball. She lives in the United States.	Use *the* with musical instruments but not with sports. Use *the* when a country's name includes *United* or *Kingdom* or ends with a plural –*s*.

> ◆ **Question 8 Using No Article for a Whole Category in General**
>
> In English, it is correct to say *the tiger is a mammal,* but it is not correct to use the definite article *the* and mean the same thing in *the tigers are mammals.* Why is it not possible?

This question is about how English speakers refer to a whole category of a thing in general. The first example is about the more general category (*mammal*) that a species (*tiger*) belongs to. The second example refers to a specific group of tigers.

Consider these four sentences. Sentences 1 and 3 are singular. Sentences 2 and 4 are plural.

Sentence	Pattern
1. **A tiger** is a big animal.	*a* + NOUN
2. **Tigers** are big animals.	NOUN + *–s*
3. **The tiger** is a big animal.	*the* + NOUN
4. **The tigers** are big animals.	*the* + NOUN + *–s*

Only Sentences 1, 2, and 3 can be used to mean all tigers in general. In everyday English, 1 and 2 are common. Sentence 3 is used more often in science material found in a book or on a website.

Sentence 4 is grammatically possible but different in meaning from the other three sentences.

If you look up an animal such as *tiger, camel,* or *chimpanzee* on Wikipedia or a similar website, you can see the variation in article usage.

The short answer to this question is that it is not OK in English to use *the* + plural noun to refer to a whole category or class. When someone says *I like the Toyotas that are parked over there,* that person is referring to specific cars. If the person wants to talk about liking that kind of car in general, however, the sentence could be *I like Toyotas because they are sturdy* or *I like a Toyota because it gets really good gas mileage,* but use of the plural noun *Toyotas* (or *cats* or *vegetables*) without *the* is more common.

• Question 9 *the* with Days and Months

Can I say *the Monday*? For example, My first class begins *the Monday*. What about months? Can I say *the January*?

In English, *the* is not used with days of the week or months of the year. Therefore, **the Monday* and **the January* are wrong.

This error is most likely due to first language interference. A Spanish speaker is likely to say **the Monday* because a Spanish speaker must say **the Monday* (*el lunes*). A Japanese speaker would probably not make this mistake since the days of the week do not have *the* in Japanese (*getsuyoubi*). (Japanese has no definite or indefinite articles.)

English requires *the* before a specific Monday, such as *the Monday after New Year's Day* or *the last Monday in June*.

• Question 10 *the* with Country Names

Why do you say in English *the* Philippines, *the* Netherlands, *the* United States of America, and *the* United Kingdom, but you cannot say *the Korea, the Japan,* or *the Russia*? Is there any good explanation to this?

The vast majority of country names do not use *the*. However, in English, *the* is used for names of countries that sound plural, including countries that end in –s or have the words *United* or *Union*. In addition, English also uses *the* with a country name that includes the words *Republic, Kingdom*, or a similar term.

Reason for *the*	Examples
with –s	the Philippines the Netherlands the United States (the U.S. or the U.S.A.)
with *United* or *Union*	the United Arab Emirates (the U.A.E.) the United Kingdom the Soviet Union
with *Republic* or *Kingdom*	the Dominican Republic the Kingdom of Saudi Arabia

◆ Question 11 *the* with Geographic Areas

Do we use *the* with parts of the world? For example, why do
we say *the* equator instead of *equator*?

In English, *the* is used with certain geographic terms but not with
others. There is no easy way to predict which words use *the* and
which do not.

Use *the* with	Examples
many regions or areas	the Middle East, the Northwest, the South, the East Coast, the West, the Lowlands, the Midwest, the Western Hemisphere
parts of our planet	the equator, the Arctic, the North Pole, the International Dateline
parts of our universe	the universe, the sun, the moon
groups of mountains	the Alps, the Andes, the Himalayas
deserts	the Sahara, the Mohave Desert

Do NOT use *the* with	Examples
continents or similar divisions	Europe, southern Europe, Latin America, Southeast Asia
states or similar divisions (provinces, departments, prefectures)	California, Ohio, Ontario, British Columbia, Antioquia (a department in Colombia), Guangdong (a province in China)
cities	New York, Paris, Cairo
planets	Saturn, Venus, Mars Exception: Earth or the Earth
an individual mountain	Mount Everest, the Himalayas

2: Articles ◆ **15**

◆ Question 12 *the* with Bodies of Water

Do we use *the* with bodies of water in English? You say *the* Pacific Ocean but not *the Lake Michigan*. Is there a rule here?

Most bodies of water use *the*, but a few do not. Use *the* with rivers, oceans, and seas. Note that even without including the type of body of water in the name, use *the*. For example, we can say *the Pacific Ocean* or *the Pacific*.

Do not use *the* with individual lakes. However, *the Great Lakes* uses *the* because it is plural.

Use *the* with	Examples
rivers	the Mississippi River, the Nile River
oceans	the Pacific Ocean, the Atlantic Ocean
seas	the Mediterranean Sea, the Caspian Sea
canals	the Panama Canal, the Suez Canal
gulfs	the Gulf of Mexico, the Arabian Gulf

Do NOT use *the* with	Examples
lakes	Lake Superior, Lake Victoria, Beaver Lake
bays	Biscayne Bay, Hudson Bay

Besides lakes, other smaller bodies of water that do not use *the* include ponds, creeks, brooks, and bayous; however, these bodies of water are very rare in general English usage. Good teachers always consider their students' language needs first. Will your students need to talk about a named pond, a named creek or brook, or a named bayou? That depends on the topography of the area where they live, but the chances are low. Will your students even need the words *pond, creek,* or *bayou* in Academic English? The most likely answer is a no, so teachers should not even introduce any information about these three relatively rare bodies of water in that case.

◆ **Question 13** *the* with Schools

Do I use *the* with a university? a college? What about a
school? I say *the University of Michigan,* but why don't people
say *the Michigan State University.*

The answer here is relatively simple. If the name of the place includes
a prepositional phrase with *of,* then we usually use *the* before it: *the
University of Michigan.* However, if there is no phrase with *of,* the
word *the* is not necessary: *Michigan State University.*

This pattern of using *the* when there is a prepositional phrase
beginning with *of* also applies to universities, colleges, and schools.
The type of educational institution does not matter.

The names of most elementary schools, middle schools, and high
schools do not include an *of*-phrase.

Program	no *the*	*the*
university	Harvard University Boston University	the Massachusetts Institute of 　Technology the University of Southern 　California
college	Colorado College Smith College	the College of New Jersey the College of William and Mary
school	Bay Elementary School Boone High School Frankfurt International 　School	the High School of Glasgow the International School of 　Minnesota the American School of Bangkok

---

◆ **Question 14** *the* **with Buildings, Monuments, and Parks**

In English, which places need the article *the* in front? Do I stay at *Hilton Hotel* or *the Hilton Hotel*? Do I visit *Miami Zoo* or *the Miami Zoo*?

The is used with most hotels (*the* Marriott), museums (*the* Louvre), art galleries (*the* National Gallery), libraries *(the* Carnegie Library*)*, and monuments (*the* Lincoln Memorial, *the* Eiffel Tower).

At the same time, there are some places that do not require *the*, including most rail stations (Union Station), airports (O'Hare), parks (Central Park), and churches (Notre Dame).

In English, the names of most zoos use *the*, especially those using the names of cities: *the* Miami Zoo and *the* Bronx Zoo.

◆ **Question 15** *the* **with People's Titles**

Why is it correct to say *the President* but not *the President Obama*?

With a person's name after their title, do not include *the*. However, use *the* when the noun is used without the person's name. For example, *President Bush met Prince Charles in London* is correct; it is not correct to say **The President Bush met the Prince Charles in London.*

In some languages (Spanish, Arabic, French, and German), it is OK to use *the* with a person's title. For instance, a Spanish speaker in a class in Mexico might say *El profesor Lopez va a llegar a las 8*, but in English **The professor Lopez is going to arrive at 8* is not correct.

In English, *the* is not used with a person's name: **the Michael* or **the Michael's book.* This second error is a possible one by Spanish, French, or Italian speakers.

Similarly, do not say **the God*, which is a possible error by Arabic speakers.

3 ◆ Clauses

A clause is a group of related words that has a subject and a verb. In English, there are three kinds of clauses.

An **adjective clause** describes a noun (or pronoun):

> The title of the book <u>that I am reading</u> is *Along the River Always*.

An **adverb clause** tells when, where, how, why, how much, and under what conditions:

> I will call you <u>if my flight is delayed</u>.

A **noun clause** is a clause tells what or who:

> The police reported <u>that someone broke into the store</u>.

3 Common ESL Errors with Clauses

ESL Error	Explanation
1. *We watched a movie who lasted for almost three hours.	Learners may use the wrong pronoun. In adjective clauses, *who, that,* and *whom* are used for people and *that* and *which* are for inanimate objects.
2. *Because the first location was not suitable for a large group.	An adverb clause is not a complete sentence. This error is called a **fragment**, which can be a serious problem in writing.
3. *Can you tell me where lives Mrs. Miller?	Students sometimes use incorrect word order in a noun clause.

What is an adjective clause? Sometimes my writing teacher writes on my essays, "You need to use more adjective clauses."

An **adjective** is a word that describes a noun (or pronoun), and a **clause** is a group of related words that has a subject and a verb. Therefore, an **adjective clause** is a clause that describes or gives more information about a noun. In other words, an adjective clause does the same job as an adjective.

Adjective clauses are useful in speaking or writing because they help us combine information into one longer sentence. In short, we are putting the information from one clause into the other clause.

clause 1	The food was delicious.
clause 2	The children ate the food.
sentence with adjective clause	The food <u>that the children ate</u> was delicious.

In addition, using adjective clauses adds variety to English writing. Using only **simple sentences** would make the writing less interesting.

The placement of adjectives and adjective clauses is different. An adjective usually comes immediately <u>before</u> the noun. In contrast, adjective clauses go <u>after</u> the noun.

Adjectives	Adjective Clauses
I like my <u>new</u> car.	The car <u>that I bought</u> was not expensive.
I do not have an <u>expensive</u> car.	I bought a car <u>that was not expensive</u>.

A **relative pronoun** is the pronoun that usually begins an adjective clause. The most common relative pronouns are *who, whom, that,* and *which.*

In general, *who, whom,* and *that* can be used for people, and *that* and *which* can be used for inanimate things.

Other possible relative pronouns include *where, when,* and *whose.*

Relative Pronoun	Examples
who	A driver <u>who runs a red light</u> may get a fine.
that	The only South American country <u>that is bigger than Argentina</u> is Brazil.
which	Not many tourists visit Jacksonville, <u>which is the largest city in Florida</u>.
whom	If you have a question about visas, the person <u>whom you need to see</u> is Mr. Jenks.
where	When I was a kid, my family moved to an area <u>where it rained almost every day</u>.
when	In the movie *Titanic*, many people cry at the moment <u>when the ship sinks</u>.
whose	A famous Argentinean <u>whose name many foreigners know</u> is Eva Peron.

◆ **Question 17 Omitting *that* in Adjective Clauses**

a. *The book that Yusif bought is really good.*

b. *The book Yusif bought is really good.*

Which is correct? Is the word *that* OK here? Is it correct without the word *that*? My computer program put a green wavy line under *that* to tell me to check it. Do the two statements have the same meaning? Why do I see both forms?

An **adjective** clause often begins with the **relative pronoun** *that* or *which* if the clause describes a thing, such as *book.* If the adjective clause describes a person, it can begin with the relative pronouns *who, whom,* or *that.* (See Question 16 for more examples.)

There is a very clear grammar rule here. If the relative pronoun is a subject of the clause, you can never omit it because every **conjugated** verb must have a subject.

When the relative pronoun is the subject, it can never be omitted:

> **The book** that is on the table **belongs** to Yusif.
> **S1**   S2 V2   **V1**

In this example, the word *that* is the subject for the verb *is* and cannot be omitted.

If the relative pronoun is the **direct object** of the verb in the clause, then it can be omitted. If we use *that* instead of *whom,* which is usually possible, or *who* instead of *whom,* which is common in informal language, then these relative pronouns can also be omitted because it is generally possible to omit the pronoun if it functions as the direct object.

In the example from this student's question, *The book that Yusif bought is really good*, the main sentence is *The book is really good* and the adjective clause is *that Yusif bought*.

<u>**The book** *that* *Yusif* *bought* **is really good**</u>.
S1   S2   V2   **V1**

Let's look at how this sentence with an adjective clause was formed.

1. We start with two sentences that have a repeated word or concept (*the book*).

    a. The book is really good.
    b. Yusif bought ~~the book~~.

2. We do not want to repeat the noun *book* twice, so we replace one noun with a pronoun. Because *book* is a thing, we use *that* to substitute for book.

    b. Yusif bought that

3. The pronoun is moved to the beginning of the adjective clause. Relative pronouns begin most adjective clauses.

    b. that Yusif bought

4. The adjective clause is then inserted inside the first sentence immediately after the noun that it describes (*book*).

    a. *The book (that Yusif bought) is really good.*

Because the word *that* is not the subject of the adjective clause, however, the pronoun *that* can be omitted: *The book Yusif bought is really good*. Remember that subject relative pronouns have to remain, but object relative pronouns are optional.

Both of these sentences express the same meaning, and, in terms of grammaticality, both are equally acceptable. Neither is better than the other.

◆ **Question 18 Adjective Clauses Modifying a Sentence**

Here's an example I heard yesterday with the word *which*:
Maria asked my brother if she could borrow his car, but he said he wouldn't lend it to her, <u>which</u> made her really mad. I hear this kind of sentence all the time. Is this OK?

This group of words beginning with the word *which* is called an **adjective clause**. While adjective clauses come <u>after</u> that noun they modify, the adjective clause here is modifying the whole sentence.

An adjective clause can describe the **subject** of a sentence, the **direct object** of a sentence, or the **object of a preposition**. In these sentences, the adjective clauses are in parentheses.

subject	The <u>man</u> (who is holding a dog) owns two cats. ↓ **subject**
direct object	Our teacher explained three underlined <u>words</u> (that were in the paragraph). ↓ **direct object**
object of preposition	We are studying about a <u>war</u> (that lasted a century). ↓ **object of preposition**

In addition to these traditional examples of what an adjective clause can describe in a sentence (i.e., subject, direct object, object of preposition), there is at least one other possible use of an adjective clause: to describe a whole sentence.

This structure is much more common in conversation or informal language.

- The weather caused all the flights to be late today, *which made people angry.*
- Last night I ate a lot of chocolate cake, *which means this week I need to exercise more.*

Notice that these adjective clauses that describe the whole sentence or situation all come at the end of the statement, all begin with the word *which*, and all have a comma before them.

What is the purpose of these end-of-sentence adjective clauses? In most cases, this type of adjective clause expresses an opinion of what happened in the sentence. By adding an adjective clause beginning with *which*, the speaker is making a comment or giving an opinion about the content of each sentence.

Consider the first example: *The weather caused all the flights to be late today, which made people angry.* First, the speaker states a fact: *The weather caused all the flights to be late today.* After that, the speaker adds extra information that includes a personal observation: *which made people angry.*

In this kind of adjective clause that makes a comment about the whole sentence, the relative pronoun *which* is the only possible option. *That* cannot replace *which* in these settings.

Note that not all *which* clauses modify the whole sentence, however. In *This morning I ate scrambled eggs and toast, which is what I eat almost every morning,* the *which* clause is modifying the nouns *scrambled eggs and toast.*

◆ Question 19 Extra Object Pronoun in Adjective Clauses

My teacher crossed out the word *it* in this sentence that I
wrote: *Mozzarella is a delicious cheese that everyone should eat
~~it~~.* Why is *it* wrong here?

This question is about adjective clauses. The short answer is that
the pronoun *it* is already expressed by the word *that*, so *it* is unnec-
essary. This type of error is usually made by speakers of Arabic or
Farsi (Persian), who are translating from their native language.

First, let's look at how **adjective clauses** are formed.

1. We start with two sentences that have a word or concept
   that repeats.
   a. *Mozzarella is a delicious* <u>cheese</u>.
   b. *Everyone should eat this* <u>cheese</u>.

2. The word *cheese* is repeated, so we cross out the second
   example of *cheese*.
   b. *Everyone should eat ~~this cheese~~.*

3. Adjective clauses use the pronouns *who* or *that* for people
   and *that* or *which* for things, so we change *cheese* to *that*.
   b. *Everyone should eat* <u>that</u>.

4. The pronoun is moved to the beginning of the adjective
   clause.
   b. <u>that</u> *everyone should eat.*

5. The adjective clause is now inserted into the main sentence.
   The adjective clause should go after the noun it describes.
   That word is *cheese*.
   a. *Mozzarella is a delicious cheese* <u>that everyone should eat</u>.

In our new sentence, the pronoun *that* means *cheese*. Thus, we
already have the word *cheese* and we have a pronoun (*that*) substituting for *cheese*. In English, we do not need another pronoun (*it*)
for *cheese*.

◆ Question 20 Embedded Questions/Noun Clauses

Why is it wrong to ask, *Do you know what time is it?*

The correct form of the question is *Do you know what time it is?*
In English, there are two ways to form a yes/no question:

invert the subject and verb	He is a good student. → *Is he a good student?* You can go. → *Can you go?* They have gone home. → *Have they gone home?*
use a form of the auxiliary verb *do*	You have a car. → *Do you have a car?* She speaks Greek. → *Does she speak Greek?* It rained last week. → *Did it rain last week?*

In the student's question, the last part (*what time is it*) is not the real question. The real question is, *Do you know* (something)? This sentence uses an **embedded question**, which is a type of noun clause.

When you embed, or put, a ***wh–* question** into another sentence, the word order for that *wh–* question changes to statement word order: **question word + subject + verb.**

Question	Embedded Question
What time <u>is</u> <u>it</u>? *wh–* V S	I don't know what time <u>it</u> <u>is</u>. *wh–* S V
Where does <u>Cindy</u> <u>live</u>? *wh–* *do* S V	No one knows where <u>Cindy</u> <u>lives</u>. *wh–* S V
When <u>will</u> <u>Jo</u> <u>arrive</u> here? *wh–* V S V	Do you know when <u>Jo</u> <u>will arrive</u>? *wh–* S V

It does not matter if the new sentence is a statement (*I don't know what time it is*) or a question (*Do you know when the next bus will arrive?*); the word order in the embedded clause will always be **question word + subject + verb.**

Sometimes the question word is also the subject: *I don't know <u>who</u> took the keys.*

◆ Question 21 Reported Speech

What is reported speech?

Reported speech, which is also called indirect speech, is the use of a reporting verb such as *say, explain,* or *announce* to tell what someone said. An example is *Timmy said he had a headache.* This sentence uses reported speech to summarize this **direct speech**: *Timmy said, "I have a headache."*

Reported speech is a little difficult because it requires knowing how to change the verbs. To make this change, shift the tense of the main verb back one tense earlier (in time). Therefore, the verb *have* in the original message *I have a headache* became *had* because present tense will change to past tense. (One tense earlier in time than the present is the past.)

Examples of Verb Shift in Reported Speech		
	Direct Speech	**Reported Speech**
simple present → simple past	She explained, "I'm hungry."	She said (that) she was hungry.
will → would	Jenny said, "I will drive there on Friday."	Jenny said (that) she would drive there on Friday.
present progressive → past progressive	Tina said, "I'm not sleeping enough."	Tina said (that) she was not sleeping enough.
should, could, would, must, might, ought to, used to → no change	Mark said, "My dad should work less."	Mark said (that) his dad should work less.

In addition to changes in verb tenses, there are some vocabulary changes, especially with time words, place words, and pronouns.

> Direct speech: Nikki said, "I want to eat dinner here."
> Reported speech: Nikki said (that) she wanted to eat dinner there.

In this example, notice how the verb *want* changes to *wanted*, the word *here* changes to *there*, and the pronoun *I* changes to *she*.

In addition to tense shift, another difficulty with reported speech is word order.

A simple way to think about **reporting verbs** is in two categories: verbs that act like *say* and verbs that act like *tell*.

say	Subject + reporting verb + (*that*) + subject + verb.
	He said (that) he would go.
tell	Subject + reporting verb + indirect object + (*that*) + subject + verb.
	He told me (that) he would go.

Verbs that behave like *say*: *admit, agree, announce, claim, explain, mention, promise, say, suggest.*

Verbs that behave like *tell*: *convince, inform, notify, persuade, remind, tell.*

In academic writing, citing other people's ideas often requires the use of reporting verbs and is an important component of good academic writing.

♦ **Question 22 Hypothetical *if* Clauses**

If I had $20,000 right now, I would buy a new car. I think this sentence is talking about the present. That's what I think *right now* means. I don't understand how you can use *had* here because *had* is past tense, and this sentence is talking about the present. Is this correct?

Verbs after *if* use a special structure called the **subjunctive mood** when the action after *if* is unreal, hypothetical, or imaginary.

In a **conditional** sentence that talks about a hypothetical condition at the present time, English speakers use what looks like past tense for the *if* clause, but it really is subjunctive. Therefore, English speakers say *If I had, If I could, If I knew*, etc.

The only verb that is a bit different is *be*. The past tense of *be* is *was* and *were*, but in subjunctive, *were* is used for all subjects. Thus, it is correct to say *If I were you, I wouldn't do that* or *If English were easier, more people would learn it more quickly.* (In very informal language, people often say *If I was you . . .* and *If English was. . . .* In formal or academic English, *were* is correct.)

The other verb in the sentence is in the result clause, and it usually has the form: *would/could* + verb. Consider these examples:

Present Situation	Unreal Conditional Sentence about Present Time
A. I want to buy a new car. I don't have $20,000.	B. If I **had** $20,000, I **would buy** a new car. unreal present condition, unreal result
C. I want to call Sam. I don't know his number.	D. If I **knew** Sam's number, I **would call** him. unreal present condition, unreal result
E. I want to change things, but I am not the president.	F. If I **were** the president, I **would change** things. unreal present condition, unreal result

One of the most common uses of the subjunctive is in *if* clauses. Another common use is after the verb *wish*, which is a structure that is very common in spoken English: *I wish I had a million dollars right now.*

Present Situation	Unreal Clause after *Wish*
I don't have a million dollars.	I wish I **had** a million dollars.
I live far from my office.	I wish I **didn't live** so far from my office.

Some students may be discouraged by the use of grammar terminology such as subjunctive mood. How much terminology you use or don't use with your students is up to each teacher. If you think that using this type of terminology (*subjunctive*) will confuse your students, then just label this form *past*. In this particular case, I have never found using the label *subjunctive* very helpful, so I avoid it as excessive grammar labeling that is likely to confuse most students. However, some upper-intermediate or advanced students may appreciate knowing this term. In addition, a few students may already know it, so you should be prepared to talk about it if they bring it up.

◆ Question 23 *will* in *if* Clauses

I learned that I can't use *will* in an *if* clause to talk about a future condition, so I can't say *If I will study harder, my grades will improve.* I'm supposed to use present tense and say *If I study harder, my grades will improve.* The other day I heard a native speaker say *If you will lend me $100, I will pay you back in a few days.* Is this sentence okay? Why? Or why not?

It is true that it is usually not possible to use *will* in the *if* clause part of a normal future conditional sentence, so English speakers do not say **If I will study more, my grades will improve.*

Sometimes it is possible to use *will* in an *if* clause, but the meaning is different. Using *will* in this case means "if you agree to do this." (It's where the adjective *willing*, as in *Are you willing to do that?* comes from.) Thus, when the speaker said, *If you will lend me $100, I will pay you back in a few days,* he or she is saying that if the listener agrees to lend the money, then he or she will pay that person back. It is a kind of negotiation.

Here are some other possible examples:

1. If you *will* clean the kitchen, I will clean the bathroom.
2. If the hotel manager *will* reduce the weekly price, we can stay there for a whole week.

Here are some examples where it is NOT possible:

3. *If it *will* rain tomorrow, we will stay home. (The rain can't make a promise.)
4. *If your plane *will* be late, I will pick you up at the airport. (The plane can't agree.)

4 ◆ Connectors

Connectors (or **conjunctions**) join words, phrases, clauses, and sentences. The choice of which connector to use depends on meaning and function. To give additional information, we can use *and, in addition,* or *moreover.* For a contrasting idea, use *but, however,* or *conversely.* To explain a time relationship, use *before, after,* or *while.* For a cause-effect relationship, use *because, if,* or *therefore.*

Connectors also vary in linguistic function. To connect two **independent clauses**, use a coordinating conjunction such as *and, but,* or *or.* To introduce a **dependent clause**, use a subordinating conjunction such as *although, because,* or *unless.*

There are several types of connectors:

- ◆ **coordinating conjunctions:** *and, but, or, so, nor, yet, for*
- ◆ **subordinating conjunctions:** *after, although, as, as long as, because, before, if, since, so, so that, though, whatever, whenever, while, unless, until*
- ◆ **correlative conjunctions:** *both . . . and, either . . . or, neither . . . nor, not only . . . but also, whether . . . or not*
- ◆ **conjunctive adverbs:** *accordingly, also, consequently, finally, furthermore, however, indeed, instead, meanwhile, nevertheless, similarly, still, subsequently, therefore, thus*

3 Common ESL Errors with Connectors

ESL Error	Explanation
1. *We went to Paris last year, we had a very good time.	Many writers, even native speakers, omit the connector.
2. *Canada is the second largest country in the world, however it ranks only 38th in population.	Many writers, even native speakers, use the wrong punctuation for connectors.
3. *Although a flea is a tiny insect, but its bite can be very painful.	Some ESL learners use two connectors to connect two ideas, but only one is possible.

◆ Question 24 Beginning a Sentence with *and*

Is it OK to begin a sentence with the word *and*?

In formal academic writing, it is usually not OK to write a sentence that begins with *and*. Sentences that begin with *and* appear in news articles or in novels, which is different from academic writing.

In academic writing, it is still generally not acceptable to begin a sentence with *and* or any of FANBOYS, which is the acronym representing the seven **coordinating conjunctions** of English: *for, and, nor, but, or, yet, so*. Coordinating conjunctions connect words, phrases, clauses, or sentences of equal rank.

- The new immigration law is complex **and** controversial.

  adjective +*and*+adjective

- The new immigration law is complex, **and** many people disagree with its intent.

  clause   +   *and*   +   clause

In conversation, however, it is fairly common to hear *and* or *but* at the beginning because it connects the second speaker's idea to the first speaker's idea. In other words, the two speakers have made one sentence together.

Sarah: I told the police officer that I wasn't speeding.

Paula: **And** what did he say?

It is OK to start a sentence with *and* in email because it is often more like a conversation than formal writing.

Your ESL students may one day have in a class where the instructor is not bothered by written sentences starting with *and*, but students should first learn not to start sentences with FANBOYS. Later they can modify their writing depending on the guidelines given by their instructor.

◆ **Question 25 Punctuation of** *but, although, however*

If *but, although,* and *however* have a similar meaning of "contrast between two different ideas," why is their punctuation so different?

All three words have a similar meaning. All three have a similar job in a sentence: to show the contrast or difference between two ideas.

All three are connectors, but they are different types of connectors. Each of these three types of connectors requires different punctuation.

Coordinating conjunctions (*and, but, for, nor, or, so, yet*) do not belong to either clause:

> Alaska is huge**, but** it has a relatively small population.
>
> S + V   **, but** S + V

Subordinating conjunctions (*after, although, as long as, because, now that, once, since, unless, until, when, while*) are part of a dependent clause. When a dependent clause begins a sentence, it is followed by a comma:

> **Although** he was only 17, Robert Heft designed the U.S. flag.
>
> **Although** S + V   ,   S +   V

When a dependent clause comes after the independent clause, there is no comma:

> Robert Heft designed the U.S. flag **although** he was only 17.
>
> S +   V   **although** S + V

When *while* is used to contrast ideas, a comma is often needed:

> Some languages have tenses, while others have none.
>
> S +   V   **, while**   S +   V

Conjunctive adverbs (*consequently, furthermore, however, moreover, nevertheless, therefore*) use either a semicolon and a comma, or they can use a period and a comma:

> <u>Apple pie is</u> delicious**; however,** <u>it has</u> many calories.

> S + V   **; however,** S + V

> <u>Apple pie is</u> delicious. **However,** <u>it has</u> many calories.

> S + V   **. However,** S + V

Both options are correct.

A related error involves including two connectors in the same sentence. A common example is with *although*: *Although the restaurant was crowded, but the service was fast.* Teachers should tell students to keep only one connector for the two clauses. In this sentence, we can keep *although* (*Although the restaurant was crowded, the service was fast*) or *but* (*The restaurant was crowded, but the service was fast*). This error is especially common among Chinese learners of English.

◆ Question 26 *though*

Why do I hear people say *though* at the end of a sentence so much? What is the correct way to use this word?

The word *though* is very similar in meaning to the word *although* or *even though*. All three items are used to connect two contrasting or different ideas. All three can occur between two clauses, and all three can occur at the beginning of a sentence.

- ◆ *Although* the report is difficult to read, it is very interesting.
- ◆ *Though* the report is difficult to read, it is very interesting.
- ◆ *Even though* the report is difficult to read, it is very interesting.

The word *though* is much more common than *although* or *even though*, especially in speaking. In the Corpus of Contemporary American English (COCA), *though* occurs 219,673 times, while *although* occurs only 137,436 times and *even though* only 46,224 times, as of the writing of this book. These frequency counts tell us that the word *though* is 60 percent more common than *although* and almost 500 percent more frequent than *even though*, which is why a student might notice it so much in English.

In conversation, *though* usually occurs at the end of a spoken sentence, so logically it tends to stand out: *I can't spell that word. I know what it means, though.* At the end of a sentence, *though* often contrasts with the information given in the previous sentence.

Location	Example	Notes
beginning (note the commas)	*Although* this car comes with leather seats, many cars do not offer that option. *Even though* this car comes with leather seats, many cars do not offer that option. *Though* this car comes with leather seats, many cars do not offer that option.	When *although, though,* and *even though* begin a sentence, a comma separates the two clauses.
middle	This car comes with leather seats *although* many cars do not offer that option. This car comes with leather seats *even though* many cars do not offer that option. This car comes with leather seats *though* many cars do not offer that option.	When *although, even though,* and *though* connect two clauses in the middle, no comma is needed.
end	This car comes with leather seats. Many cars do not offer that option, *though.*	Only *though* can go at the end of a sentence. This pattern is very common in spoken language. A comma is often used just before *though.*

5 ◆ Gerunds & Infinitives

A **gerund** is a verb form that ends in –*ing* and functions as a noun. An **infinitive** consists of *to* + verb. To form a gerund or an infinitive, simply add –*ing* at the end or *to* at the beginning.

A gerund can do several things in a sentence. It can be the subject (*Washing my car is hard*), the direct object (*I hate washing my car*), or an object of a preposition (*I'm tired of washing my car every Friday*).

An infinitive has three main jobs. As an adverb, it can give a reason (*I went there to buy a cake*). As a noun, it can be a direct object after a verb (*I want to buy a cake*). The infinitive in the first sentence tells why I went there, and the infinitive in the second sentence tells what I want to do. As an adjective, it describes a noun (*My decision to leave was correct.*). (An infinitive as subject is possible but not common: *To choose a new car takes a lot of patience.*)

Many ESL learners make errors with gerunds and infinitives after certain verbs. In the example *I want to travel more*, we use an infinitive (*to travel*) because the verb *want* requires an infinitive. In the example *I enjoy traveling*, we use a gerund (*traveling*) because the verb *enjoy* requires a gerund.

3 Common ESL Errors with Gerunds and Infinitives

ESL Error	Explanation
1. *Olivia needs buy new shows.	Learners sometimes use the base form of a verb instead of an infinitive after certain verbs such as *need*.
2. *Carl should to take care of his health.	Students often use an infinitive instead of the base form of a verb after a modal (*can, should, may*).
3. *Make tuna salad is easy.	Students often use the base of a verb instead of a gerund in the subject position.

♦ Question 27 Gerunds

What is a gerund?

A **gerund** is a word that ends in the suffix *–ing*, came from a verb, and is now used as a noun. Even though it ends in *–ing* and may look like a verb, a gerund is always a noun.

Because a gerund is a **noun**, it can do anything a noun can do. Therefore, it can be the subject of a sentence, the direct object of the verb, or the object of a preposition.

In these three examples, *walking* is a gerund:

Example	Function of *walking*
Walking a mile every day is good for my health.	the subject
Most people enjoy *walking* along the beach.	the direct object
Some people are afraid of *walking* barefoot outside.	the object of the preposition *of*

It is important for learners to know that the verb form used after a preposition should be a gerund: *Are you interested in going tomorrow?* A gerund is also used after a **phrasal verb**: *We should put off buying a car.*

It is important for students to know that that not every word ending in *–ing* is a gerund. A word that ends in *–ing* can also be an adjective (*This is an interesting book*) or a verb in a **progressive**, or continuous, tense (*We are driving to northern Michigan tomorrow*).

For those who want to know specific grammar labels, an *–ing* form used as an adjective or as part of a verb tense is called a **present participle**. However, this label is not helpful to many learners.

◆ **Question 28 Verb + Gerund**

In English, you say *I want to go, I need to go,* and *I hope to go,*
so why do you say *I enjoy going?* Why do you say *I enjoy going*
instead of *I enjoy to go?*

◆ **Question 29 Verb + Infinitive**

In English, people say *I should go, I can go,* and *I might go,* so
why do people say *I want to go?* Why is *I want go* not possible?
Why do you need *to?*

The underlying question here is which word form comes after a
certain verb. In English, some verbs are followed by a gerund (*enjoy,
avoid, finish*), some verbs by an infinitive (*want, need, hope*), and
some modals (*should, can, might*) are followed by only the base form
of the verb. Here are three examples of how the first verb (*enjoy,
want, should*) controls the form of the next word:

verb + gerund	verb + infinitive	verb + base form
I *enjoy* going to school.	I *want* to go to school.	I *should* go to school.

The use of *enjoy going* instead of **enjoy to go* has to do with the verb
that comes before *going* or *to go: enjoy.* The first verb controls the
form of the following word.

Here is a partial list of some verbs that can be <u>followed by a
gerund</u>: *admit, avoid, can't help, complete, consider, deny, detest,
dislike, enjoy, finish, get through, imagine, mind, miss, postpone,
practice, quit, resist, risk, spend (time), suggest, tolerate, waste (time).*

Here is a partial list of some verbs that can be <u>followed by an
infinitive</u>: *agree, ask, decide, demand, deserve, expect, hesitate, hope,
intend, know (how), learn, manage, need, offer, plan, prepare, pretend,
promise, wait, want, wish, would like.*

There are no general rules that say that one kind of verb is followed by a gerund while another kind of verb is followed by an
infinitive. However, students can learn these patterns by memorizing, hearing, or seeing them many times.

Native speakers did not memorize these patterns. Instead, they have acquired them through repeated exposure to these verbs in natural contexts. Most English learners, unfortunately, do not have this luxury of time or exposure to such rich contexts, so memorizing the most frequent and most useful verbs is an excellent plan of study.

A longer list of verbs followed by gerunds (and verbs followed by infinitives) is available in Key 10 of Chapter 3 in *Keys to Teaching Grammar to English Language Learners, 2nd Edition* (Folse, 2016).

What specifically should students do with a longer list? A bad strategy is to try to learn all the verbs without the learners thinking of their actual English needs. In contrast, the smartest specific strategy English learners can follow is to look over these longer lists and identify a smaller number, say five or ten, of verbs that they really believe they need for their own English. They should then memorize those verbs followed by a correct form of any common verb. For example, if students think they need to know the verbs *decide* and *avoid* for their English purposes, then they should memorize useful phrases such as *decide to leave* and *avoid eating* because perhaps they can imagine having to say *So we decided to leave early* or *My doctor told me to avoid eating bread*. They should never just memorize a grammar rule such as "The verbs that are followed by gerunds are *admit, avoid, can't help,* etc."

If learners cannot imagine using the verbs *deny, resist,* and *urge* or *deserve, hesitate,* and *manage*, then they should skip those verbs and concentrate on more practical verbs. Always encourage your students to think of their actual English needs with this and all grammar rules. One quick way to determine whether a verb is common is to do a search in a **corpus** that is relevant to your students' needs, such as the **Corpus of Contemporary American English (COCA)**.

✦ Question 30 Infinitives and Gerunds after Certain Verbs

Which is correct: *I stopped drinking coffee* or *I stopped to drink coffee?*

Both are correct, but the meanings are very different. *I stopped drinking coffee* means that I no longer drink coffee today. *I stopped to drink coffee* means that I stopped some action, such as driving a car, in order to drink coffee. In fact, *to* in this example is actually a shortened form of *in order to*. A common student error is the use of *for*: **I stopped for drink coffee.* Using *for* + verb is never correct.

In sum, a **gerund** after the verb *stop* is the action that you no longer do (*I stopped drinking coffee*), but an **infinitive** after the verb *stop* tells why you stopped some other action (*I stopped to drink coffee*).

Some verbs are <u>followed by an infinitive only</u>. *I want to go* is correct—never **I want going.* Other verbs followed by an infinitive include *decide, expect, hope, need, promise,* and *would like.*

Some verbs are <u>followed by a gerund only</u>. *I enjoy going* is correct—never **I enjoy to go.* Other verbs followed by a gerund include *avoid, finish, mind, miss, quit,* and *spend (time).*

However, there are other verbs that can be followed by either an infinitive or a gerund. With verbs such as *forget, remember,* and *stop,* the meaning changes. With other verbs such as *begin, continue,* and *like,* there is no difference in meaning.

Information about verbs followed by infinitives and gerunds appears in Key 10 of Chapter 3 in *Keys to Teaching Grammar to English Language Learners, 2nd Edition* (Folse, 2016). This information includes a longer list of verbs that can be followed by either an infinitive or a gerund with no change in meaning as well as a list of those with a change in meaning.

What should students do? The smartest strategy is to identify the verbs in each group that they really believe they will need. They should then memorize those with the correct verb form that follows. For example, if students think they need to know the verbs *decide, avoid,* and *begin* for their English purposes, then they should memorize useful examples such as *decide to leave, avoid eating, begin to rain,* and *begin raining,* etc.

Verb + Infinitive Verb + Gerund (different meanings)	Verb + Infinitive Verb + Gerund (similar meanings)
forget infinitive: *I forgot to buy a tie.* • This means I did not buy the tie. I did not remember to do it. gerund: *I forgot buying that tie.* • This means I bought the tie but could not remember the action. Maybe my credit card bill had a note that said "Tie Shop $20.52," but I was surprised when I saw the bill because I could not remember spending $20.52 at the Tie Shop.	**begin** infinitive: *Suddenly it began to rain.* gerund: *Suddenly it began raining.*
remember infinitive: *I remembered to buy salt today.* • This means I bought salt at the store today. I did not forget to do it. gerund: *I remember buying salt, but where is it?* • This means I have the memory of buying salt, but it's not in this bag with the other groceries I bought.	**continue** infinitive: *Unfortunately, it continued to rain.* gerund: *Unfortunately, it continued raining.*
stop infinitive: *I stopped to call my boss.* • This means I called my boss. I stopped another action such as driving in order to make this call. gerund: *I stopped calling my boss.* • This means I do not call my boss any more.	**like** infinitive: *I like to play tennis at night.* gerund: *I like playing tennis at night.*

◆ **Question 31** *ask, tell, want* **and Similiar Verbs**

Maria wants that I make the cookies. What is wrong with this sentence?

In English, we do not use *that* + subject + verb after the verb *want* and certain other verbs. The correct sentence is *Maria wants me to make the cookies.* After the verb *want*, you can never have a subject and a verb. Therefore, you can never say **I want that a taxi takes me to the airport.*

The most basic sentence in English is subject + verb + **direct object**. For example, a beginner might say *She wants some cookies*: *She* (subject) + *wants* (verb) + *some cookies* (direct object).

It is also possible to make a more complex sentence by adding more information. It is possible to include a second action (verb) in the sentence to talk about the cookies. For example, will she *buy* the cookies? Will she *make* the cookies? Will she *eat* the cookies?

If you include these three verbs after the verb *want*, you have to use an **infinitive**.

Idea 1	Idea 2	New Sentence with an Infinitive
She wants some cookies.	She buys the cookies.	She wants **to buy** some cookies.
She wants some cookies.	She makes the cookies.	She wants **to make** some cookies.
She wants some cookies.	She eats the cookies.	She wants **to eat** some cookies.

In the three new sentences, one person does both actions. In all three cases, the subjects for both actions are the same person.

Now imagine the same three situations, but imagine that she is not able to buy the cookies, make the cookies, or eat the cookies herself. Instead, she wants Matt to do these three actions. In all three cases, the subjects for both actions are now different people.

In these cases with different people, the new sentence has this pattern: subject + verb + **indirect object** + infinitive. (Another way to view this is that the indirect object is functioning as a sort of second subject, but it uses the object pronoun form. Thus, we would say *She wants him to buy the cookies*, but not **She wants he to buy the cookies*.)

Idea 1	Idea 2	New Sentence with Indirect Object and Infinitive
She wants some cookies.	He buys the cookies.	She wants <u>him</u> to **buy** the cookies.
She wants some cookies.	He makes the cookies.	She wants <u>him</u> to **make** the cookies.
She wants some cookies.	He eats the cookies.	She wants <u>him</u> to **eat** the cookies.

The three new sentences have different meanings from the original three. Here are possible explanations:

- She wants him to buy the cookies = because she cannot go to the store now.
- She wants him to make the cookies = because she doesn't know how to make cookies.
- She wants him to eat the cookies = because she knows he really loves cookies.

Only certain verbs behave like *want*. Here are some common verbs that can follow this same pattern of subject + verb + indirect object + infinitive:

Subject + Verb + Indirect Object + Infinitive		
advise	get	prefer
allow	help	recommend
ask	invite	teach
cause	need	tell
encourage	order	urge
expect	permit	want
force	persuade	would like

The most important thing to remember here is that most of these verbs <u>cannot</u> be followed by *that* + subject + verb. For example, **I want that you help me* is never possible.

Among ESL learners, **I want that you* + verb is a very common error because it is a direct translation from some languages, including Spanish, Portuguese, French, and Italian.

♦ **Question 32** *let, make, have,* and *help*

The verbs *allow, permit,* and *let* have similar meanings. If I can say *He allowed me to use his car* and *He permitted me to use his car,* why can't I say *He let me to use his car?*

These three verbs have very similar meanings, but the grammar of words with similar meanings can often be different.

After the verbs *allow* and *permit,* an object and an infinitive are possible. They are similar to the verbs *want* and *need.*

Subject	Verb	Object	Infinitive	Other Information
He	*allowed*	me	*to use*	his car.
He	*permitted*	me	*to use*	his car.
He	*wanted*	me	*to drive*	his car to the airport.
He	*needed*	me	*to put*	gas in his car.

The verb *let* is different. After the verb *let,* we put the object and then the second verb. However, the second verb uses the base form. It has no *–s,* no *–ed,* no *–ing,* and no *to.* Two other verbs that behave the same way are *have* and *make.*

Subject	Verb	Object	Base Form	Other Information
He	*let*	me	*use*	his car.
He	*made*	me	*drive*	his car.
He	*had*	me	*wash*	his car.

Let, make, and *have* are called **causative verbs** because they cause someone to do something. All three of these causative verbs follow the same sentence pattern of subject + verb + indirect object + verb.

Another way to view this is that the indirect object is functioning as a sort of second subject, but it uses the object pronoun form. Thus, we say *He made me do my homework,* not **He made I did my homework.*

The verb *help* can also follow this same pattern, but it can also use an infinitive. There is no difference in meaning between these two patterns.

Subject	Verb	Object	Base Form	Other Information
He	*helped*	me	*learn*	the information.

Subject	Verb	Object	Base Form	Other Information
He	*helped*	me	*to learn*	the information.

The key here is to draw students' attention to the form of the second verb that follows the four causative verbs. The base form has to be used after *let, make,* and *have.* After *help,* either the base form or infinitive can be used with no difference in meaning.

6 ◆ Prepositions

Prepositions are small words that show a relationship between words in a sentence. They connect the noun after them (that is, the **object of the preposition**) to the other information in the rest of the sentence. There are three types of prepositions, according to the number of words in each.

1-word prepositions	*about, after, at, before, by, for, in, of, on, with*
2-word prepositions	*according to, due to, far from, instead of*
3-word prepositions	*in addition to, in back of, in front of, on top of*

Sometimes the use of a certain preposition makes sense. When I say *My money is in my wallet,* we use *in* because the money is <u>inside</u> the wallet. We cannot see the money now. Everyone understands why we use *in* here.

At other times, the use of a certain preposition does not make sense. In English, Mary gets married *to* Joe, but in Spanish, French, Japanese, Arabic, and other languages, Mary gets married *with* Joe, not *to. With* means "together," and the two people are now together, so doesn't *with* seem more logical?

3 Common ESL Errors with Prepositions

ESL Error	Explanation
1. *We will travel to Brazil on August.	Many students often confuse *in* and *on*.
2. *My English class is in Tuesday.	
3. *I am afraid from spiders.	Sometimes learners do not know which preposition to use after a certain adjective.

◆ Question 33 *at/on/in* for Location

Is there a rule for which preposition to use with a place? Should I say *at Canada* or *in Canada*? Should I say *on Main Street* or *in Main Street*?

There are three main prepositions that are used for location: *at, on, in.* Although these three can be confusing, there is a rather simple explanation.

The choice of preposition depends on the type of location. More specific places use *at*, while larger places tend to use *in*. *On* is for streets (or similar words such as *avenues* or *highways*).

Type of Location	Examples
an address with a house number	I live <u>at</u> 2251 Walnut Street.
the name of a business or similar	We ate lunch <u>at</u> Burger King. I study <u>at</u> the University of Oregon.
a street (or similar)	I live <u>on</u> Walnut Street. The bank is <u>on</u> Park Avenue. The school is <u>on</u> Highway 92.
a city, a state, a province, a country, a neighborhood	We have a park <u>in</u> my neighborhood. I live <u>in</u> Montreal. Montreal is <u>in</u> Quebec. Quebec is <u>in</u> Canada.

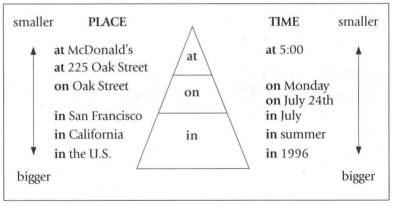

From *Clear Grammar 2, 2nd ed.* (Folse, 2012), p. 269. University of Michigan Press.

◆ **Question 34** *at* + **Time**

Do you say *at 12 o'clock* or *in 12 o'clock*? Which one is correct and why?

In English, we use the preposition *at* to name the time, so we say *at 12 o'clock*. This is true even if it is a time word or phrase, such as *at noon*.

Numbers	Words
at 12 PM	at noon
at 12 AM	at midnight
at 7:45	at a quarter to eight
at 7:30	at seven-thirty
at 11:59 PM	at the last minute
at 2:23 AM	at the last moment

◆ **Question 35** *on* + **Days**

Do you say *on Monday* or *in Monday*? Which is correct? Why?

In English, we can use the preposition *on* to name a day or a date, so we say *on Monday*. It can be one of the seven days of the week, but it can also be a specific date, such as *on June 3rd* or *on my birthday*.

We also say *on the weekend*, which is logical because the weekend consists of days.

Days	Dates
on Monday	on August 17, 1989
on Tuesday	on my birthday
on Saturday	on the last day of June
on the weekend	on the 16th

Another question that comes up about the days of the week is the use of the **definite article** *the*. Some learners, especially speakers of Spanish and French, incorrectly say *My first class begins on the Monday, *My first class begins in the Monday,* or *My first class begins the Monday* because these languages use *the* with days.

The correct sentences are *My first class begins Monday* or *My first class begins on Monday.* With days of the week, we do not use *the.* You can use *on* or no preposition; it is optional. However, we do not say **the Monday* unless you are referring to a specific Monday, such as *I flew to Miami on the Monday after my birthday.*

◆ **Question 36** *in* + **Months**

Do you say *on January* or *in January*? Which one is correct? Why?

In English, we use the preposition *in* to name months, so we say *in January* and *in March.* We also use *in* with any time measurement that is bigger than a day, so we use *in* with weeks, months, seasons, years, decades, and centuries.

weeks	months	seasons	years	decades	centuries
in week 2	in June	in winter	in 1999	in the 1980s	in the 1800s
in the third week	in March	in summer	in 2017	in the '60s	in the tenth century

♦ **Question 37 Prepositions after Certain Adjectives**

In English, why do you say *Mark is married to Olivia*? In my language, we say *Mark is married with Olivia*. How do I know which preposition (*to* or *with*) to choose?

In English, the adjective *married* is always followed by the preposition *to*. One piece of advice is to learn *married to* as one phrase, not two separate words.

If I put my keys inside a box and you cannot see them now, we say *The keys are in the box*. Here, the preposition *in* has the meaning of "inside." If we change the word *box* to *table*, then we cannot say *The keys are in the table* because that is impossible. We have to say *The keys are on the table*. In these examples, the word <u>after</u> the preposition (*box, table*) makes a difference.

Now consider the example *We are very interested in that movie*. Here, the preposition *in* does not have the meaning of "inside." If we change the word *movie* to *book* or *car* or *candidate* or *idea*, we still say *in*. In these examples, the word after the preposition does not make any difference. The word that matters here is the word <u>before</u> the preposition, which is the adjective *interested*. In English, *interested in* is an adjective + preposition combination that students should learn.

There are many adjectives in English that are usually followed by a specific preposition. ESL students need to learn the most common adjective + preposition combinations. Here is a short list of adjective + preposition combinations. A much longer list can be found in Key 6 in Chapter 3 in *Keys to Teaching Grammar to English Language Learners, 2nd Edition* (Folse, 2016).

Adjective + Preposition Combinations		
afraid of	far from	proud of
angry about	full of	ready for
angry at	good at	sick of
certain about/of	guilty of	similar to
confused about	interested in	sorry about
embarrassed by	known for	surprised at/by
excited about	married to	tired of
famous for	okay with	worried about

◆ Question 38 *in* / *on* + Transportation

Why do you say *in a car* but *on a bus*?

The choice of the preposition *in* or *on* depends on the mode of transportation.

We use *in* with cars of any kind. We can travel *in a car, in a taxi,* and *in an ambulance.* We use *on* for everything else.

in	*on*	
a car	foot	a train
a taxi	a bicycle / a bike	a plane
a cab	a motorcycle	a boat
a truck[1]	a subway	a ship
an ambulance	a bus	a truck[1]

It is often possible to use the preposition *by* with modes of transportation, so we also say *I went by car* or *When she leaves the office every day, she goes home by bus.* However, when you use *by,* you do not add any other information. For example, you cannot say **I went by my own car* or **When she leaves the office every day, she goes home by bus 71.* You should say *I went in my own car* and *When she leaves the office every day, she goes home on bus 71.*

---

[1]Both *in a truck* and *on a truck* are possible, but they are different types of trucks. When it is a truck that an average person might drive (like a pick-up truck), it is correct to say *I drove to work in my truck.* However, when it is a large truck often used for commercial purposes (like a semi or 18-wheel tractor trailer), it is correct to say *Food usually travels between cities on a truck.*

◆ Question 39 *at / in* with Schools and Hospitals

Which is correct: *at school* or *in school*?

Both *at* and *in* are correct, but their meanings are different.

When you use *at*, it refers to location. When you use *in school*, it refers to being a student. Therefore, the principal is *at school*, but a high school student is *in school*. The phrase *in school* has a broader context than the phrase *at school*.

at school	*in* school
Caller: Can I speak with Jill?	Caller: Where is Jill working now?
Mother: I'm sorry, but she's not here right now. She's *at school*. She should be home by 5 PM.	Mother: Jill isn't working anywhere because she's still *in school*. She graduates in one more year.
Meaning: Jill is at school right now.	Meaning: Jill may or may not be at school right now, but she is a student.

The phrase *in school* can be any kind of school. To talk specifically about a college or university, speakers of American English use *in college*, even if the student attends a university. (British English tends to prefer *university*.)

The noun *hospital* functions in a similar way. When you say *at a hospital*, it describing where a person is. However, when you say *in a hospital*, it refers to receiving care there. Therefore, a doctor works *at a hospital*, but a person who is very sick is *in a hospital*.

In North American English, no article is used with *school*, but we use *a* or *the* with *hospital*. British English does not use an article with either: *in school, in hospital*. (See Question 100.)

♦ Question 40 Prepositions after Verbs of Motion

I hear people say *I'm going home*. Why is it *go home*? We say *go to class* and *go to Mexico*, so why not *go to home*?

The correct expression is *go home* and not **go to home*. This is a very common error made by all English learners.

With verbs of motion, the word *home* has no preposition before it. With other verbs that do not show motion, prepositions may be required.

Verbs of Motion	Other Action Verbs
I'm *going* home now.	We're *eating* dinner <u>at</u> home tonight.
She *arrived* home around noon.	On Mondays, I often *work* <u>at</u> home.
She *got* home around noon.	With fast internet speed, I can *work* <u>from</u> home.
Let's *walk* home.	
If I *drive* home, it will take ten minutes.	*Amelia Bedelia* is a good book for children to *read* <u>at</u> home.
Her children *fly* home every summer.	The salesperson said he would *demonstrate* the vacuum <u>in</u> my home.
Can I *take* this book home?	

Other places that do not usually take prepositions include *here, there, downtown, upstairs*. Japanese speakers may say **I will go to there*, which is a direct translation from Japanese. Spanish speakers may say **Let's go to the downtown,* which is a direct translation from Spanish.

◆ **Question 41** *in* vs. *into*

What's the difference between *in* and *into*? Are they interchangeable?

Both *in* and *into* are prepositions. Although these two prepositions are closely related in meaning, they are different. The preposition *in* tells location, while *into* indicates movement.

	Meaning	Example
in	inside (location)	*The coins are in my wallet.*
into	toward the inside (movement)	*I put the coins into my wallet.*

In is more flexible than *into*. It is generally OK to use *in* for both meanings. Therefore, it is also OK to say *I put the coins in my wallet.* You can usually use *in* for location and movement, but it is never OK to use *into* for location.

Another way to remember this is that most examples of *into* can be written with *in*, but the reverse is not true. It is OK to say *She got into the car* or *She got in the car.* It is OK to say *I threw the paper into the trash can* or *I threw the paper in the trash can.*

It is not correct to use *into* for location. *Lima is in Peru* is correct, but **Lima is into Peru* is not. *I was born in Mexico* is correct, but not **I was born into Mexico.*

♦ Question 42 *in a group* vs. *on a team*

Why is *in a team* wrong? In English, you say *in a group*, so why do you say *on a team*?

In some cases, prepositions are idiomatic. They simply do not seem to make much sense. They just have to be learned in the new language.

The concepts of *group* and *team* are similar in meaning, but these two words use different prepositions. Using two different prepositions with two words that have very similar meanings may seem irrational and random, but prepositions are problematic in most languages.

In English, we say *in a group*. For example, a teacher might say to her class, "Students, today we're going to work *in three different groups*. Students who are *in the first group* will make a list of idioms with animal names. Students *in the second group* will make a list of idioms with color words. The students *in the third group* will make a list of idioms with food words. I'd like the students *in each group* to choose one person to write your final list on the board." Notice that the preposition *in* occurs before group or groups five times.

In English, we say *on a team*. If you want to know about the number of players for a sport, you might ask these questions: *How many players are on a baseball team? How many players are on a soccer team? How many players are on a basketball team? How many players are on a football team?*

These two words once again remind us that prepositions are by far one of the most difficult problems for anyone learning a new language. One useful strategy is to ask students to memorize the preposition usages that are most important for their language needs. Prepositions can be tricky, so all teachers need to pay attention to prepositions in phrases and sentences that are important for your learners' needs.

Searching for a list of prepositions on the internet will produce a list, but many of these lists are far too long and contain prepositions that are uncommon (*unto*) or archaic (*abaft*). For a list of useful prepositions for English learners, see Key 6 in Chapter 3 in *Keys to Teaching Grammar to English Language Learners, 2nd Edition* (Folse, 2016).

7 ◆ Pronouns

Pronouns take the place of nouns. Therefore, they can have the same grammatical functions as a noun. They can be a subject (*We have a new house*), direct object (*The cat saw us and ran away*), indirect object (*Jill gave us the money*), or object of a preposition (*This present is for us*). There are several types of pronouns:

- ◆ **subject pronouns:** *I, you, he, she, it we, they*
- ◆ **object pronouns:** *me, you, him, her, it, us, them*
- ◆ **relative pronouns:** *who, that, which*
- ◆ **indefinite pronouns:** *anyone, anything, anybody, everyone, everything, everybody, someone, something, somebody, no one, nothing, nobody*
- ◆ **reflexive pronouns:** *myself, yourself, himself, herself, itself, ourselves, yourselves, themselves*
- ◆ **demonstrative pronouns:** *this, that, these, those*
- ◆ **possessive pronouns:** *mine, yours, his, hers, ours, theirs*
- ◆ **reciprocal pronouns:** *each other, one another*

3 Common ESL Errors with Pronouns

ESL Error	Explanation
1. My favorite city is Boston. *Is a very special place to me.	Spanish and other languages often omit a subject when it is a pronoun.
2. Do you know Mr. Timwell? *I think that she is your neighbor.	Learners often confuse *he* and *she* because their language has only one word for both *he* and *she* or because *he* and *she* are similar in spelling and pronunciation.
3. Cars are important. *People need it today.	Sometimes speakers use a singular pronoun to refer to a plural noun.

◆ **Question 43 Meanings of *it***

What does the word *it* mean in English?

The word *it* is a **pronoun**. Perhaps the easiest usage to understand is that the pronoun *it* can replace a noun that names a thing: *Where is Paris? It is in in France.* In this example, *it* replaces the noun *Paris.* Most ESL students can understand this usage of *it*, but there are several other usages that are more challenging for learners.

Usage	Examples	Explanation
instead of a thing	I have a new car. It is nice.	The pronoun *it* replaces the noun *car.* Using the noun *car* again so near the first example of *car* would sound repetitive.
instead of an animal	Look at that tiger! It's huge.	The pronoun *it* replaces the noun *tiger.*
	I have a small cat. *She's* black and about six years old. *She's* very quiet.	In general, we use *he* or *she* for an animal that we know well or have a personal relationship with, such as with a family pet.
	I saw a cat outside my apartment today. *It* was all white and had a collar.	When we are talking about an animal that is not a pet or that we do not know personally, we use the pronoun *it.*
	A giraffe is a beautiful animal. *It* has a very long neck and small ears.	When we are talking about an animal in a general or scientific way, we use *it.*
for time	It's 7:15 PM.	We use *it* to talk about clock time.
	It is Monday.	We use *it* to talk about days.
	It is June 8th.	We use *it* to talk about dates.
	It's June.	We use *it* to talk about months.
	It's summer.	We use *it* to talk about seasons.
	It was 2012.	We use *it* to talk about years.

Usage	Examples	Explanation
for weather	*It*'s raining. *It*'s hot today.	We use *it* to talk about weather.
for opinions	*It*'s important to sleep at least eight hours a night.	We use *it* to give an opinion that is followed by an infinitive.
	It's good seeing you again.	We use *it* to give an opinion that is followed by a verb that ends in *-ing*.

One of the most common ESL student errors is omitting *it* when it is the subject of a sentence: *I have a new car. *Is very beautiful.* In this example, the missing *it* clearly refers to a car.

Some usages of *it* have no clear reference. This is sometimes called the **dummy subject** because English requires the main verb in every clause to have a subject even if it has no clear, specific referent. We use it as a kind of filler, or dummy, subject in this case. In the example *it is raining* and *it's important to sleep at least eight hours a night*, the pronoun *it* is not replacing a noun and has no clear referent. Its only role is to occupy a mandatory subject position.

◆ Question 44 Differentiating Formal and Informal *you*

In my language, we have two words for *you*. One *you* is for a person I know very well, and the other *you* is for a person that I do not know well or for a person with a much higher rank, such as a doctor, a professor, or an older person. We also have a singular and plural for *you*. How do I show these differences in English?

As this student indicates, some languages, such as Spanish, French, Russian, Polish, and Persian, have two different words for *you*. In Spanish, there is *usted* for formal use and *tú* for people with whom you are familiar. In French, there is *vous* for formal and *tu* for informal. Other languages, such as Japanese and Korean, have **honorifics** that indicate status through the use of **affixes** or grammatical case.

Although English has no formal grammar to distinguish between *you* singular and *you* plural, many regional variations of English do in fact make this distinction, especially in informal spoken English. In the southern U.S. states, for instance, the word *y'all* (an abbreviation for *you all*) is used routinely. In most other states, *you guys* is used, regardless of gender. In some places in the U.S., speakers say *you-uns*. These are variations, not part of standard English grammar.

This spoken distinction between singular *you* and plural *you* is not only in American English. In British English, *you lot* is used for the informal plural form. In some other places where English is spoken, *yous* and *youse* are used. Again, these are local varieties.

What should an English learner do? Your learners already have enough to worry about with English grammar, vocabulary, pronunciation, etc., so one strategy is to do nothing. For your more proficient learners, you may wish to share this information to help improve their listening comprehension. However, you may wish to stop short of encouraging them to actively use any of the regional plural *you* forms unless they have stronger proficiency.

• Question 45 *who* vs. *whom*

When do you use *whom*? When do you use *who*?

Both *who* and *whom* are pronouns that refer to a person. We use them in questions when the person or people are unknown. The difference is in grammatical usage, not meaning.

Here are the grammar rules for formal use of *who* and *whom*:

who	1. Use **who** as the subject of a sentence or clause.	*Who* lives there?
		I don't know *who* lives there.
	2. Use **who** when the main verb is *be*.	*Who* are your teachers this year?
whom	3. Use **whom** for the object of a verb.	*Whom* did you visit?
		I don't know *whom* you saw yesterday.
	4. Use **whom** for the object of a preposition.	*Whom* did you speak with?
		With whom did you speak?

In everyday conversation, the word *whom* is almost never used. In informal language, we can use *who* for all situations (subject or object). In short, use *who* in conversation, but not *whom*. In academic writing or formal language, however, the rules for the use of *whom* usually apply.

One case where *whom* is always required is immediately after a preposition. However, this word order sounds much more formal:

very formal	*With whom* did you speak?
formal	*Whom* did you speak with?
informal conversation	*Who* did you speak with?

◆ Question 46 *I* vs. *me*

When I was studying English in the U.S., I lived with an American family. I just received an email from the father that began "Greetings from my wife and I!" Is this right? I think it should be "my wife and me."

The correct phrase would be *from my wife and me.*

A simple technique to teach your students to check which form of pronoun to use is to separate the two people in the phrase. Can you say "Greetings from my wife" and "Greetings from I"? *From my wife* is possible here, but not **from I.* Therefore, **Greetings from my wife and I* is also impossible.

The reason is that the phrase *my wife and me* comes after the preposition *from,* so that means we need to use *me* because it is an object pronoun. The word *I* is a subject pronoun.

The use of the subject pronoun after a preposition is an example of a common error made by native speakers. Many people make this error because of **hypercorrection**. Because of earlier grammar instruction that focused on *X and I*, they believe that *(a person) and I* is the correct phrase no matter where the phrase is placed. They use it correctly in the subject position (*Joe and I work at the bank*) but incorrectly as a direct object (**The boss gave Joe and I a raise*) and as an object of a preposition (**The boss gave a raise to Joe and I.*)

Another new issue related to *I* and *me* is that it is becoming more common to hear people begin a sentence with *Me and*: **Me and my friend had an argument.* This is never correct. It is <u>not</u> just relaxed, informal conversation. It is in fact wrong for two very good reasons. First, in polite English you never put yourself first: *I* or *me* <u>always</u> goes after everyone else. Second, *me* cannot be the subject of a sentence because *me* is an **object pronoun**. You cannot say **Me had an argument*, so you cannot say **My friend and me had an argument* or **Me and my friend had an argument.*

This question also raises another important issue: the value of native speakers in informing a learner's English. Many people think a native speaker's English is perfect English. The truth is that native speakers usually have perfect pronunciation and excellent fluency, but not all native speakers actually speak standard English. Furthermore, even those who speak standard English and who are very educated may make certain errors. This happens in all languages, not just English.

While it is certainly useful to practice with a native speaker, the ideal teacher or conversation partner is someone who has excellent knowledge of English as a second or foreign language—regardless of their first language.

This chart presents five errors that native speakers commonly make in English. A longer list of 20 such errors can be found in Chapter 2 and Appendix A in *Keys to Teaching Grammar to English Language Learners, 2nd Edition* (Folse, 2016).

5 Native Speaker Errors That Students Should Not Use	
double negatives	wrong: *They don't want **no** more help.
	correct: They don't want **any** more help.
wrong past participle	wrong: *We should have **went** on Monday, not Friday.
	correct: We should have **gone** on Monday, not Friday.
wrong pronoun form	wrong: *Between you and **I**, I don't like him.
	correct: Between you and **me**, I don't like him.
using **me** as the subject	wrong: ***Me and my friend** had an argument.
	correct: **My friend and I** had an argument.
possessive **'s** used for plural	wrong: *That store is open seven day's a week.
	correct: That store is open seven days a week.

8 ◆ Pronunciation

This chapter focuses on pronunciation issues that are connected to grammar. Three examples of this include how to pronounce the *–s* ending and how to pronounce the *–ed* ending, as well as how to use syllable **stress** to differentiate parts of speech—the noun *object* from the verb *object*, for example.

There is one question (47) that deals with the three ways of pronouncing *–s* (/s/, /z/, /ɪz/). However, there are three separate questions (48, 49, 50) that deal with the ways of pronouncing *–ed* (48 /d/; 49 /t/; 50 /ɪd/) because students tend to ask about *–ed* much more than *–s*. The suffix *–ed* merits more attention because students often add /ɪd/ to all verbs instead of /d/ or /t/ and produce unintelligible extra-syllable non-words like **reach-ed* or **clean-ed.*

3 Common ESL Errors with Pronunciation

ESL Error	Explanation
1. *Last night I <u>watch</u> TV until midnight.	One of the most common errors is omitting the past tense suffix *–ed* for past tense.
2. *After I <u>finish-ed</u> dinner last night, I <u>listen-ed</u> to some music.	Many ESL learners mispronounce every *–ed* ending as a full syllable /ɪd/: *wash-ed* instead of *wash* + /t/ or *liv-ed* instead of *live* + /d/.
3. *My brother <u>play-s</u> basketball a lot.	Most English learners do not realize that the suffix *–s* is pronounced as /z/ much more than /s/. Pronouncing *plays* with a final /s/ produces the word *place*, not *plays*.

Many answers in this chapter use symbols in slashes from the **International Phonetic Alphabet (IPA)**. Refer to the charts in Questions 47–50.

◆ **Question 47 3 Ways of Pronouncing –s**

When you add the letter –s to a word in English, how do you pronounce it? *Cats* ends with /s/ and *dogs* ends with /z/, but *horses* adds an extra syllable /ɪz/. How do I know when to use each of the three pronunciations?

In English, –s marks the plural of nouns (*cats*), the third-person singular form (*he/she/it*) of a verb in simple present tense (*she likes*), and the possessive form (*Mary's*).

Regardless of the function of –s (or –es), this ending has three possible pronunciations: /s/, /z/, /ɪz/. These same three pronunciation options affect the plural of nouns (*cats*—/s/, *dogs*—/z/, *horses*—/ɪz/), verbs in simple present tense (*he eats*—/s/, *she needs*—/z/, *it erases*—/ɪz/), and the possessive form (*Mark's*—/s/, *Maria's*—/z/, *George's*—/ɪz/).

How do we know when to use which pronunciation? The correct pronunciation of /s/, /z/, or /ɪz/ depends entirely on the last sound of the word (as it is) before adding the plural ending.

The sound /s/ is **voiceless**, which means there is no vibration of the vocal chords when you pronounce it. We add a voiceless suffix /s/ only when the final sound of the word is also voiceless, including these five: /f/, /k/, /p/, /t/, /θ/. The final sound is important. For example, *laugh* and *sniff* both end in the sound /f/ even though their final spellings are different (–gh and –ff), so we say *laughs* with an /s/ and *sniffs* with an /s/.

The sound /z/ is **voiced**. We add /z/ when the final sound of the word is also voiced, including at least 24 sounds: /b/, /d/, /g/, /l/, /m/, /n/, /ŋ/, /r/, /ð/, /v/, and all vowels.

Words that end in a voiceless sound add the voiceless ending /s/, while words that end in a voiced sound add the voiced ending /z/.

We add an extra /ɪz/ after these 6 sounds: /s/, /z/, /č/, /š/, /ǰ/, /ž/.

Which pronunciation is the most common for –s? The answer is /z/. To test this, I put together a list of 80 names of animals compiled from other teachers' lists found on the internet, as in Key 8 in Chapter 3 in *Keys to Teaching Grammar to English Language Learners, 2nd Edition* (Folse, 2016). Of these 80 animal names, 75 percent are

/z/, only 16 percent are /s/, and just 9 percent are /ɪz/. At first glance, the fact that –s is not pronounced as /s/ may be very surprising, but when you consider that 24 ending sounds combine with /z/ but only 5 go with /s/, the results are not so surprising.

Pronunciation of –s		
Pronunciation	**Ending Sound**	**Examples**
/z/	/b/	jobs, robs, Rob's
	/d/	adds, beds, Ted's
	/g/	bags, jogs, Meg's
	/l/	balls, calls, Phil's
	/m/	hums, thumbs, Jim's
	/n/	cans, runs, Ben's
	/ŋ/	rings, sings, Ping's
	/r/	cars, cares, Peter's
	/ð/	bathes, breathes
	/v/	knives, loves, Bev's
	all 14 vowels	plays, Mary's, buys, Joe's, views, boys, laws, cows, zoos, toys
/s/	/f/	cuffs, laughs, Jeff's
	/k/	kicks, socks, Rick's
	/p/	cups, keeps, Philip's
	/t/	cats, cuts, Matt's
	/θ/	baths, myths, Keith's
/ɪz/ (+1 extra syllable)	/s/	classes, erases, Bess's
	/z/	roses, pleases, Buzz's
	/č/	teaches, watches, Mitch's
	/š/	mashes, wishes, Josh's
	/ǰ/	advantages, cringes, Paige's
	/ž/	massages

Students can feel voicing first-hand by placing their index finger lightly across the lower part of their throat and pronouncing a **voiced** sound and then its **voiceless** partner. For the voiced sound, they will feel some vibration, but not for its voiceless counterpart because the voiceless counterpart is just air moving out the mouth (/g/ is voiced and /k/ is voiceless).

◆ **Question 48 Pronouncing** *–ed* **as /d/**

For regular past tense, you add *–ed* to a verb, so *play*
changes to *played*. You write *–ed*, but what is the correct
pronunciation? Sometimes I hear my friends say *play-ed*, but I
also hear *play-d*. Which is correct?

◆_**Question 49 Pronouncing** *–ed* **as /t/**

When I write a verb in simple past tense, I add *–ed*, so *need*
changes to *needed*. My friend asked me, "What did you do
last night?" I answered, "I watched TV," but my friend said
my pronunciation of the verb *watched* was wrong because I
pronounced it as two syllables: *watch-ed*. My friend said the
–ed should be /t/, so I should say *watch-t*. Is this correct? Why
is the *–ed* pronounced /t/ and not an extra syllable as in *wanted*
(*want-ed*) or *needed* (*need-ed*)? I think *–ed* should be /ɪd/.

◆ **Question 50 Pronouncing** *-ed* **as /ɪd/**

For past tense, you add the letters *–ed*, but how do you
pronounce it? *Laughed* ends with the sound /t/ and *played*
ends with the sound /d/, but can you also say *laugh-ed* and
play-ed with two syllables? When is it ok to pronounce *–ed* as
an extra syllable /ɪd/ and when is it not?

In English, we write the simple past tense of regular verbs by adding
the suffix *–ed*, but how we pronounce it is more complicated. In fact,
there are three ways to pronounce the *–ed* ending: /ɪd/, /d/, and /t/.

Most students may believe the only way to pronounce –*ed* is as a full extra syllable /ɪd/, which is precisely how it looks. In fact, even many native speakers are not explicitly aware of the three possible pronunciations for –*ed* because native speakers have not thought about these details of their own language. They acquired this information early in childhood.

Consider these examples:

Pronunciation	Examples with Notes	
/ɪd/ (+ 1 extra syllable)	*needed*	1 syllable becomes 2 syllables
	subtracted	2 syllables becomes 3 syllables
	concentrated	3 syllables becomes 4 syllables
/d/	*played*	*play* and *played* are both 1 syllable, but many ESL learners incorrectly say the past tense as 2 syllables: **play-ed* instead of *play-d*
/t/	*danced*	*dance* and *danced* are both 1 syllable, but many ESL learners may incorrectly say the past tense as 2 syllables: **danc-ed* instead of *dance-t*.

The Pronunciation of –ed as /d/

Why do we sometimes pronounce the suffix –ed as /d/? The short answer is that it depends on the final sound of the word. If the word ends in the sounds /b/, /g/, /v/, /z/, /l/, /m/, /n/, /ŋ/, /r/, /ǰ/, /ž/, /ð/ or one of the vowel sounds, we pronounce the suffix as the sound /d/.

There is a longer linguistic reason why we use /d/ and not another ending. The sound /d/ is **voiced**, which means there is vibration of the vocal chords when it is pronounced. Other voiced sounds can be seen in the chart. We add /d/ to words that end in a voiced sound. Teachers should emphasize to students that the final sound, not the spelling, is important. For example, *glue* and *view* both end with the same sound /u/ but have very different final spellings (*–ue* and *–iew*).

Pronunciation of *–ed* as **/d/**	
Voiced Final Sound	**Possible Spellings (with Examples)**
/b/	grab → grabbed
/g/	beg → begged
/v/	live → lived
/z/	please → pleased
/l/	pull → pulled
/m/	scream → screamed
/n/	clean → cleaned
/ŋ/	belong → belonged
/r/	clear → cleared
/ǰ/	damage → damaged
/ž/	massage → massaged
/ð/	bathe → bathed
all 14 vowels	play → played agree → agreed sigh → sighed snow → snowed view → viewed

The Pronunciation of -ed *as /t/*

Why do we sometimes pronounce the suffix *–ed* as /t/? The answer is that it depends on the final sound of the word. If the word ends in the **voiceless** consonant sounds /f/, /k/, /p/, /s/, /č/ or /š/, we pronounce the *–ed* suffix as the sound /t/. The final sound, not the spelling, matters. For example, *hope* ends in the letter *–e*, but the final sound is /p/. Therefore, we pronounce *hoped* with /t/. Likewise, the word *laugh* has an odd spelling, the last letter is *–h*, but the last sound is /f/, so the past tense of *laugh* is pronounced with /t/. Final voiceless sounds add a voiceless ending /t/.

Pronunciation of *–ed* as /t/	
Voiceless Final Sound	**Possible Spellings (with Examples)**
/f/	lau<u>gh</u> → laughed photogra<u>ph</u> → photographed sni<u>ff</u> → sniffed
/k/	ki<u>ck</u> → kicked ba<u>ke</u> → baked
/p/	sto<u>p</u> → stopped ho<u>pe</u> → hoped
/s/	mi<u>ss</u> → missed
/č/	wat<u>ch</u> → watched
/š/	wa<u>sh</u> → washed

The Pronunciation of -ed *as /ɪd/*

Finally, we pronounce the *–ed* suffix as an extra syllable when the original verb ends in the sound /d/ or /t/. Therefore, words that end in /d/ (*need, end, guide*) or /t/ (*want, start, vote*) are pronounced with an extra syllable (*needed, ended, guided, wanted, started, voted*). This contrasts with words that do not end in /d/ or /t/, which in turn do not add an extra syllable (*wish* → *wished, sneeze* → *sneezed*).

Pronunciation of *–ed* as /ɪd/	
Final Sound	**Possible Spellings (with Examples)**
/d/	nee<u>d</u> → needed deci<u>de</u> → decided
/t/	wan<u>t</u> → wanted vo<u>te</u> → voted

How common is each of the three pronunciations for –*ed*? Because it is always a good idea to consider your students' actual language needs, one way to answer this is to look at the kinds of verbs that your students most likely need for their English. For example, I compiled a list of the 100 most frequent examples of verb forms ending in –*ed* from the Corpus of Contemporary American English (COCA), which is the largest freely available collection of North American English. The complete list can be found in Key 8 in Chapter 3 in *Keys to Teaching Grammar to English Language Learners, 2nd Edition* (Folse, 2016).

The chart shows that the voiced pronunciation /d/ occurs 55 percent of the time, which means just over half of all academic verbs are pronounced with /d/ in past tense. The second most common pronunciation is /t/ at 25 percent, while /ɪd/ occurs only 20 percent of the time.

Distribution of Three –*ed* Pronunciations in the 100 Most Frequent Regular Past Tense Verbs		
Voiced /d/	**Voiceless /t/**	**Extra Syllable /ɪd/**
55%	25%	20%

How can teachers help their learners? Since the most common student error in pronouncing the –*ed* ending of words is to say an additional syllable /ɪd/ for every –*ed* ending, teachers need to help learners correctly use /d/ and /t/ instead of /ɪd/. Teachers should tell their students that pronouncing every –*ed* as /ɪd/ is not a good strategy because it may result in errors 80 percent of the time, which is an unacceptable error rate that is very likely to result in miscommunication.

Teachers should teach their students about the three possible endings /d/, /t/, and /ɪd/. The easiest to teach is /ɪd/ because it is the ending students will automatically add because they will see –*ed* and then say it as a separate syllable /ɪd/. It is also the easiest because it occurs after only two final word sounds: /d/ and /t/.

Here are two examples of **word walls** with regular verbs that end in the sounds /d/ or /t/. (An irregular verb like *put* has no place here because the past form is *put*, without *–ed*. Similarly, a noun like *bed* or *cat* has no place because the goal is to be able to add *–ed* to practice final /d/ or /t/ + *–ed* = /ɪd/.)

The **word wall** on the left features high-frequency verbs that end with /d/, while the one on the right presents high-frequency verbs that end with /t/.

Words Ending with /d/	
–d	need
	end
	add
	avoid
–de	provide
	include
	trade
	decide

Words Ending with /t/	
–t	want
	start
	act
	expect
–te	complete
	create
	vote
	indicate

Learning the list of word final sounds that require the pronunciation of /t/ is also not so difficult to accomplish because there are only six: /f/, /k/, /p/, /s/, /č/, /š/.

With junior high school to adult students, this instruction can be done explicitly. Here are two examples of simple word walls with regular verbs that end in just the sound /f/.

The **word wall** at the left presents six words in alphabetical order, while the one on the right presents the same six words but organized by spelling pattern.

Spellings for /f/	
cough	laugh
graph	sniff
handcuff	telegraph

Spellings for /f/		
–gh	*–ff*	*–ph*
cough	sniff	telegraph
laugh	handcuff	graph

The group of final sounds that takes /d/ is much larger, with at least 26 sounds: /b/, /g/, /v/, /z/, /ǰ/, /ž/, /ð/, /l/, /m/, /n/, /ŋ/, /r/, and all of the 14 vowel sounds. Though you may certainly teach your students this list of 26 sounds, I think a more efficient and less taxing way would be to teach the previous two groups (sounds for /ɪd/ and sounds for /t/) first, and then you can tell your students that all other final word sounds add the sound /d/ for the suffix –ed.

Teachers may use a **word wall** to help learners master this information. For middle school, high school, and university students, here is a word wall with the top 20 –ed words with the final /d/ pronunciation (listed in frequency order as reported in COCA):

Top 20 –ed Verb Forms with Final /d/ Sound				
1. used	5. seemed	9. died	13. learned	17. showed
2. called	6. tried	10. played	14. killed	18. followed
3. turned	7. involved	11. considered	15. received	19. lived
4. happened	8. moved	12. changed	16. opened	20. (un)identified

---

◆ **Question 51 Reductions such as** *wanna*

Is it correct to say *wanna* instead of *want to*?

In English, the verb *want* can be followed by a noun (*I want a sandwich*) or an infinitive (*I want to eat a sandwich*). In informal spoken English, the words *want* and *to* can blend together and sound like one word *wanna*. Thus, you may hear people say *I wanna eat a sandwich*. In this same conversation, you might hear someone ask the question *Where do you wanna eat?* (*want + to eat*) or *When do you wanna go there?* (*want + to go*).

It is important to know, however, that *wanna* should not be used in formal or academic writing. The spoken word *wanna* is just that—spoken informal language. Some people may write *wanna* when they are texting or writing a short note to someone, but tell your students that *wanna* is never acceptable in written language unless they know the person and are in fact very good friends with that person. If the word *wanna* appears in a book, the author is trying to re-create a conversation between people who probably know each other well.

If an email is for business purposes, it is never OK to use *wanna*. For example, when applying for a new job by email, do not use *wanna* (or *gonna* for *going to* or *hafta* for *have to*). A person who responds to a job announcement by writing "I saw your ad for a manager, so I *wanna* apply for that job because I have a lot of experience in that kind of job" will probably not get that job.

In informal speaking, it is normal to say *wanna* in two situations. First, the word *want* can change to *wanna* before an infinitive. In fact, the second syllable –*na* (*wanna*) is really a reduced form of *to*. A common error is to say *wanna* plus the word *to*, as in **I wanna to go now* instead of *I wanna go*. Second, the word *want* can change to *wanna* when the next word is *a*, so students can say *I wanna new car* or *I wanna class that isn't hard*.

Give students these five sentences with *want* and ask them to decide which ones they think *wanna* is possible for in informal conversation.

1. I want to go to the bank now.
2. Do want this book?
3. Do you want to buy this book?
4. We want to talk to Jill, but she is busy.
5. We want Jill to talk to us, but she is busy.

After looking through these examples, they should have said that *wanna* is possible for Numbers 1, 3, and 4. We can say *wanna* when an infinitive follows *want* (1, 3, 4). (For more information, see Hot Seat Question 15 in Chapter 4 in *Keys to Teaching English to Speakers of Other Languages, 2nd Edition*.)

◆ **Question 52 Syllable Stress and Part of Speech**

Why does *present* have two different pronunciations? How do I know which pronunciation to use and when?

The word *present* can be pronounced two ways. All of the sounds in the two pronunciations are the same, and the only difference is in the **stress**, or emphasis, of the word.

If the first syllable is stressed, we say *PRE-sent.* This is a noun. It means "a gift." If the second syllable is stressed, we say *pre-SENT.* This is a verb. It means "to introduce or show." The general rule here is that for some two-syllable words, stressing the first syllable creates a noun and stressing the second syllable creates a verb.

12 Words That Change Grammatical Role Due to Syllable Stress			
Noun	**Meaning**	**Verb**	**Meaning**
CONduct	a person's behavior	conDUCT	to behave; to manage
CONflict	a fight or disagreement	conFLICT	to differ
CONtest	a competition for a prize	conTEST	to argue against
CONtrast	the difference between things	conTRAST	to compare the differences between things
DEcrease	a drop in amount	deCREASE	to lower the amount
DEtail	an individual part	deTAIL	to tell completely
INcrease	a rise in amount	inCREASE	to raise the amount
OBject	a thing, an item	obJECT	to disagree with
PERmit	an official document of permission	perMIT	to allow
PREsent	a gift; the current time	preSENT	to introduce or show
PROject	a large piece of work that is designed for a specific goal	proJECT	to show, to make visible
REcord	information that has been preserved in writing	reCORD	to put in writing to preserve information

In English, only about 20 words use different syllable stress to change from verb to noun. Many verbs become nouns by adding a suffix of some kind, so *educate* becomes *education* and *enjoy* becomes *enjoyment*. In a relatively few cases, the verb and noun have the same word, so you *mop* with a *mop*.

All of these examples have been pairs of nouns and verbs, but other parts of speech can be impacted, too. The adjective *PERfect* can be a verb *perFECT*, which means "to improve until something is perfect."

9 ◆ Subject-Verb Agreement

Subject-verb agreement is an important part of English grammar. The verb must agree with the subject in **number**. If the subject is singular, the verb should also be singular. If the subject is plural, then the verb should also be plural.

3 Common ESL Errors with Subject-Verb Agreement

ESL Error	Explanation
1. *Thomas Edison High School have almost 2,000 students.	Students sometimes forget to add –s to a verb in simple present tense. A third-person singular verb in simple present tense needs an –s ending.
2. *The people is angry about the new law.	Learners may think a plural noun is singular because it lacks –s. A plural verb must appear with a plural noun. Some nouns like *people* and *children* do not end in –s and are therefore less obvious.
3. *The reasons for his decision is complicated.	Many learners mistake the noun that is nearest the verb for the subject of a sentence. They are often misled by nouns that are objects of a preposition. Those nouns are never the subject of that sentence.

◆ **Question 53 Subject-Verb Agreement:** *news is/news are?*

Why do you say *the news is good* and not *the news are good?*
The word *news* ends in –s, so isn't it plural?

Nouns that end in –s (*cats, pencils, tables*) are usually plural, while verbs that end in –s (*writes, speaks, needs*) are usually singular.

The noun *news* ends in the letter –s, so it looks plural, but it is not. In English grammar, the noun *news* is singular even though it ends in the letter –s. There are other nouns that also end in –s but are singular:

Category	Examples
subjects ending in –*ics*	economics, linguistics, mathematics, physics, politics
games and activities	billiards, checkers, gymnastics
sicknesses	diabetes, measles, mumps, rabies
countries	the United States, the Netherlands
others	means, series, species

A longer list of similar words can be found on the internet, but students should not try to learn all of those words. Teachers need to look at any list, select the words that they think their students need for their English, and then teach those words followed by the word *is.* For example, teach the phrases *the news is* and *politics is.*

In addition, there are also some words that end in –s that are plural in English even though they might be singular in your students' language. Three examples are *pants, glasses,* and *scissors.* We often use the phrase *a pair of* with these three nouns. For *pants,* for example, we would say *this pair of pants is* but *these pants are* even though we are referring to just one item of clothing.

◆ **Question 54 Intervening Prepositional Phrases**

From a test: 11. According to recent information, an important export of Brazil, Colombia, and Mexico ~~are~~ *is* closely connected to daily life across the globe.

I missed this question on my test. Why is my answer wrong? We are talking about three countries, so why do you write *is*, not *are*?

There are three countries in this sentence, but to choose the correct verb form, we need to find the subject of the sentence. A **subject** has to be a noun (or pronoun), so which nouns do we have before the verb that could be the subject? We have three possible options: *information, export,* and the list of three countries (*Brazil, Colombia, Mexico*).

It is easy to focus on the list of three countries because most people attempt to make the verb agree in number with the nearest preceding noun. However, the noun just in front of the verb is not always the subject.

In this example, the three country names are preceded by the preposition *of*. Therefore, these three nouns (*Brazil, Colombia, Mexico*) are objects of the preposition *of*. In English, a noun as **object of a preposition** cannot also be the subject because a noun can have only one grammatical job in any given sentence. Thus, it can be the subject or it can be the object of a preposition, but it cannot do both jobs.

In this example, the noun *information* is the object of the preposition *according to*. Therefore, it already has a grammatical job in this sentence, so *information* cannot also be the subject.

This leaves us with the noun *export*, which is in fact the subject of this sentence. Therefore, the verb should be *is*, the singular form, because the noun *export* is singular.

> *11. ~~According to recent information,~~ an important **export** ~~of Brazil, Colombia, and Mexico~~ is closely connected to daily life across the globe.*

> =

> *11. . . . an important **export** . . . is closely connected. . . .*

A useful strategy to teach students is to cross out the prepositional phrases before the verb in longer sentences when determining if the verb should be singular or plural. To practice this strategy, students should draw a line through any prepositional phrases that come before the verb. After doing this, it should be easier for them to find the subject.

◆ **Question 55** *There is a lot* vs. *There are a lot*

I read this sentence about Mexico: *For tourists, there is a lot to do in Mexico City.* I think the verb should be *are* instead of *is* because this sentence means there are many things that tourists can do in Mexico City.

The quantity word *a lot* can be singular or plural, depending on the words after it.

A lot of people <u>are</u> here.	**people** = plural noun, so we use *are*
A lot of information <u>is</u> necessary.	**information** = singular non-count noun, so we use *is*

This rule is true for *a lot of* + noun, but the question is not about *a lot of* with a noun after it. The question is about *a lot* plus an **infinitive**. In this case, the verb is always singular.

> *there + is + **a lot** +* infinitive

- *For tourists, there is* **a lot** *to do* *in Mexico City.*

- *At the picnic yesterday, there was* **a lot** *to eat.*

The quantity word *much* functions in a similar way:

> *there + is + **much** +* infinitive

- *There is* **much** *to see* *in London.*

- *In my mathematics class, there is* **much** *to learn.*

In these examples, all of the verbs are singular (*is* or *was*) because we are talking about one indefinite quantity.

The only way to use a plural verb is if the pronoun *there* refers to a plural noun before it, as with the noun *shoes* in this example:

> *This store has so many <u>shoes</u> for sale. There are a lot to choose from.*

In this example, *a lot* clearly refers to *shoes*, which is a plural word. However, when there is no previous noun mentioned, use a singular verb (*is* or *was*). Therefore, the pattern without a noun is *there + is/was + a lot/much +* infinitive.

♦ Question 56 *None is* vs. *None are*

Is the pronoun *none* singular or plural? Which is correct: *None is* or *None are*?

There are two ways to answer this question. One follows what traditional rules tell us to do, and the other describes what people actually do with this grammar question.

According to **prescriptive grammar**, *none* is always singular. The rationale is that the word *none* means "not one." *Two* is plural and *one* is singular, so zero, or *none*, should also be singular. You should say *none of the food is delicious* and *none of the books is interesting.*

According to **descriptive grammar**, however, *none* with a **non-count noun** can be singular (*none of the food is delicious*), but *none* with a plural noun can be plural (*none of the books are interesting*), which is contrary to the traditional prescriptive grammar rule. (The words *all, most,* and *some* follow the same pattern.)

If you do an internet search of whether *none* takes a singular or plural verb, you will see a variety of answers.

Language changes over time, so what should teachers tell students? The safest strategy is to tell students that in academic writing and formal language, *none* is singular. However, in informal conversation, *none* can be singular or plural, depending on the noun that it is referring to.

> ◆ **Question 57** *either . . . or* and Other Correlative
> **Conjunctions**
>
> In the sentence, *Either the cookies or the cake smells like vanilla,*
> why do you use a singular verb *smells* when you're talking
> about two food items?

The rule for subject-verb agreement with *either . . . or* is that the
verb always agrees with the subject that is closest to the verb. In
the student's sentence, the two subjects are *cookies* and *cake*. The
subject closest to the verb is the word *cake.*

> Either the cookies or the **cake** *smells* like vanilla.

We can also change the order of the subjects, but this will change
the verb:

> Either the cake or the **cookies** *smell* like vanilla.

In the second sentence, *cookies* is the subject closer to the verb, so
we use the plural verb *smell.*

Three frequently used correlative conjunctions are *either . . . or,*
neither . . . nor, and *both . . . and.* Subject-verb agreement with correlative conjunctions can be a little difficult.

Correlative Conjunction	Rule for Subject-Verb Agreement	Examples
either . . . or	The verb agrees in number with the subject that is closer to the verb.	a. *Either* you *or* Ann <u>is</u> responsible for paying the bill. b. *Either* Ann *or* you <u>are</u> responsible for paying the bill.
neither . . . nor	The verb agrees in number with the subject that is closer to the verb.	a. *Neither* you *nor* Ann <u>is</u> responsible for paying the bill. b. *Neither* Ann *nor* you <u>are</u> responsible for paying the bill.
both . . . and	The verb is plural.	a. *Both* you *and* Ann <u>are</u> responsible for paying the bill. b. *Both* Ann *and* you <u>are</u> responsible for paying the bill.

With *both . . . and,* it is logical that the subject is plural because the word *both* implies plural. However, with *either . . . or* and *neither . . . nor,* subject-verb agreement depends on the subject that is closer to the verb. If that subject is singular, the verb is singular. If that verb is plural, the verb is plural.

Notice how the second subject agrees in number with the verb *have* or *has*:

> Neither China nor **countries** in South America *have* a high number of tornadoes.

> Neither countries in South America nor **China** *has* a high number of tornadoes.

♦ Question 58 Collective Nouns

We learned that the word *family* is singular, so I should say, "My family is in New York now." On a news website, however, a famous athlete said, "My family are behind my decision to retire next year." I thought *family* was a singular noun, so it should go with *is,* not *are.* Which one is right?

Both sentences are possible. In North American English, some **collective nouns** like *family* are singular, while in British English, they are sometimes plural. During a football game, a New Yorker would say *My team is winning,* while a Londoner might say *My team are winning.* (See Question 100.)

In North American English, sometimes collective nouns like *team, audience, couple,* and *committee* can use a singular verb or a plural verb, depending on whether the speaker wants to focus on the group as one unit or the individuals of the group.

Sentence with *Committee*	Meaning
The *committee* is meeting at 7 PM.	The committee members are doing this together. I am talking about one group.
The *committee* are in disagreement about the new proposal.	I am talking about the individual members of the committee. Some like the proposal, while others dislike it.

10 ◆ Suffixes

This chapter covers a wide variety of **suffixes** that are very common in English. Some have grammatical roles (*–ing* can create a verb form in the progressive tenses), while others have semantic jobs (*–er* can create a noun that means "a person who does something").

Because the functions of these suffixes vary so much, students' errors do as well. Some of these errors are fairly basic, but others are more complicated.

3 Common ESL Errors with Suffixes

ESL Error	Explanation
1. *When I was walk home yesterday, I found some keys.	It is common for ESL students to omit *–ing* and *–ed* from verbs.
2. *I'm so boring in that class.	ESL students confuse the adjective forms that come from verbs, particularly the distinction between *–ing* and *–ed*.
3. *There are many reason why I want to learn English.	Some ESL writers forget to add *–s* to a noun to make it plural, especially when the noun is in the middle of a sentence. This is often not from lack of knowledge but rather lack of editing or **automaticity.**

How do I make a noun plural? When do I add *–es* instead of just *–s*?

The most common way to write the plural form of a noun is to add *–s*: *book → books; problem → problems; idea → ideas; building → buildings.*

Add *–es* if the noun ends in these letters: *–ch, –sh, –x, –s, –ss, –zz.*

–ch	1 sandwich → 2 sandwiches; a watch → many watches
–sh	1 wish → 3 wishes; a dish → some dishes
–x	1 box→ 2 boxes; a tax → multiple taxes
–s	1 bus → 2 buses; a gas → many gases
–ss	1 class → 2 classes; a glass → some glasses
–zz	1 buzz → 2 buzzes

A spelling rule for plural nouns is that if a word ends in a consonant and *–y*, the *–y* changes to *–i* and we add *–es*: *1 city → 2 cities; 1 baby → 2 babies; 1 lady → 2 ladies.* If a word ends in a vowel and *–y*, we just add *–s*: *1 day → 2 days; 1 boy → 2 boys; 1 guy → 2 guys.*

Words that end in *–o* present a special situation. Most words ending in *–o* simply add *–s* (*pianos*), but some add *–es* (*tomatoes*), and a few can add either (*volcanos* or *volcanoes*).

–s	photos, radios, tacos, avocados
–es	heroes, potatoes
–s or *–es*	buffalos/buffaloes, mosquitos/mosquitoes, zeros/zeroes, tornados/tornadoes

Another spelling rule for plural nouns is that some nouns that end in *–f* or *–fe* change to *–ves* in plural: *1 leaf → 2 leaves; 1 shelf → 2 shelves; life → 2 lives; 1 knife → 2 knives.*

A few nouns have an irregular plural form. The question for any teacher is which of these are worth spending time on in class. Teachers should determine which words are actually of value for students. No one knows your students' English needs better than you do, so it is up to you to decide which irregular noun forms should (and should not) be presented to your students. For example, consider the nouns *children* and *oxen*. Both are examples of irregular noun plurals in English. However, the word *children* is a very commonly used noun, while *oxen* is not. Likewise, knowing that *foot* changes to *feet* is probably more valuable than knowing the same about *goose* and *geese*.

Here is a list of some irregular noun plurals that are frequently used in English and therefore worth teaching:

	Singular	Plural
different forms	a child	2 children
	a man	2 men
	a woman	2 women
	a foot	2 feet
	a tooth	2 teeth
	a person	2 people
same forms	a fish	2 fish
	a sheep	2 sheep
	a deer	2 deer

There are a few other irregular plural forms for nouns, but they are not common and should not be the focus of a student's attention: *1 mouse → 2 mice; 1 ox → 2 oxen; 1 goose → 2 geese; 1 louse → many lice; 1 cactus → 2 cacti; 1 appendix → 2 appendices.* If you can think of a practical reason that your students need to know one of these irregular noun plurals, then teach it. However, students should learn useful language, not just grammatical rules, so very few learners need to know *geese* or *cacti*. Remember that we are not training future English linguists, so our goal is never to teach grammar forms merely because they exist. If students do not need a certain form, then do not teach it.

Non-count nouns do not have a plural form. In English, words such as *information, homework,* and *luggage* are considered non-count and do not have plural form: **informations, *homeworks, *luggages, *advices, *researches.*

◆ **Question 60 Meanings of –*ing* at the End of a Word**

When a word ends in –*ing*, what does it mean?

Most people know that –*ing* is used with verbs for actions that are happening right now, as in *I am reading this sentence now.* However, –*ing* has several other functions in English.

In English, the suffix –*ing* has at least three distinct jobs:

Functions of –*ing*	Examples	Meaning
1. a present participle of a regular verb in one of the six progressive tenses:	Kim is *working* at Chase.	action in progress
• present progressive	am/is/are *working*	
• past progressive	was/were *working*	
• future progressive	will be *working*	
• present perfect progressive	has/have been *working*	
• past perfect progressive	had been *working*	
• future perfect progressive	will have been *working*	
2. a present participle used as an adjective	Chapter 7 is the most *confusing* part of the book.	the noun modified is causing the feeling
3. a gerund (which is always a noun)	*Flying* here today took about four hours.	the name of the action

From these examples, it should be clear that –*ing* can do much more than just indicate an action that is happening right now. It can also be an adjective or a noun. Thus, this one suffix can be three different parts of speech: verb, adjective, noun.

◆ Question 61 Meanings of –s at the End of a Word

In English, a lot of words end in –s. Does it always mean plural of nouns?

The suffix –s at the end of a noun indicates plural. However, the suffix –s has three main jobs in English:

Functions of –s	Examples
1. the plural of a noun	1 *cat*, 2 *cats*
2. the ending for a verb in simple present tense when the subject is *he, she,* or *it* (third-person singular)	I *sing* well, but Kim *sings* better.
3. the possessive of a noun when there is also an apostrophe (*'s* or *s'*),	Ann's book my parents' wedding

Most nouns form the plural by adding –s, but other spellings include –es or –ies.

Second, the –s can also be the ending for a verb in third-person simple present tense: *he works, she works, it works.* The same information for –y (only after a consonant letter) changing to –ies (*try, tries*) and –o changing to –oes (*go, goes*) is true for verbs as well.

Finally, the suffix –s can be used in the possessive form of either a singular noun or a plural noun if we include an apostrophe: *That boy's shoes are for running. Those boys' shoes are for running.*

Occasionally I have been asked about –s in **contractions** such as *Mark's here.* In this case it is a contraction of two words, not a separate function.

◆ **Question 62 Meanings of –ed at the End of a Word**

When a word ends in –ed, what does it mean?

Most people know that –ed is for past tense (of regular verbs), but –ed has several other usages in English. A word ending in –ed can be simple past tense or it can be the **past participle** form of a verb. As a past participle, it can be part of the perfect tenses, part of **passive voice**, or an adjective.

In English, the suffix –ed has four main jobs:

Functions of –ed	Examples
1. the past tense of regular verbs	Yesterday I *painted* the kitchen.
2. the past participle of a regular verb in one of the perfect tenses (present perfect, past perfect, future perfect)	Kim *has worked* here since 2011.
3. the past participle of a regular verb in passive voice	The game of basketball *was invented* in 1891.
4. the past participle of a regular verb used as an adjective	My favorite food is *fried* rice.

From these examples, it should be clear that –ed can do much more than just form the past tense of verbs.

◆ Question 63 Meanings of –ly at the End of the Word

What does –ly at the end of a word mean?

Adverbs

By far, the most common function of the suffix –ly is to form an **adverb** from an adjective: *quick → quickly; careful → carefully; perfect → perfectly.*

Four exceptions here are *fast, lately, hardly,* and *well.*

- The adverb form of the adjective *fast* is *fast.* It does not change. Some beginning students often write the word **fastly.*
- The adjective *late* has the same adverb form: *He arrived late.* The word *lately* is an adverb that means "recently." The adjective *late* usually has a negative meaning, but the adverb *lately* is not negative.
- The word *hardly* is an adverb that means "scarcely, only a little," such as in *She could hardly walk after the accident.* It is not connected to the adverb *hard.* The adverb form of the adjective *hard* is *hard*: *She is a <u>hard</u> worker. She works <u>hard</u>.*
- The adjective *good* changes to the adverb *well.*

When these –ly adverbs modify a verb, they usually tell the manner in which something has been done. In other words, they answer the question "How"?

When I asked Jackie to help, she *quickly* <u>said</u> no.

The adverb *quickly* modifies the verb *said.* This is how she said it.

It's been raining a lot, so please <u>drive</u> *carefully.*

The adverb *carefully* modifies the verb *drive.* This is how you should drive.

When these –ly adverbs modify an adjective or another adverb, they usually tell the degree to which something has been done. In other words, they answer the question "to what extent"?

When the room was *completely* <u>dark</u>, the movie began.

The adverb *completely* describes the adjective *dark.*

In comparison, a turtle moves *extremely* <u>slowly</u>.

The adverb *extremely* describes the adverb *slowly*.

In the Corpus of Contemporary American English (COCA), 15 common *–ly* adverbs (in order of frequency) include:

1. *really*	6. *absolutely*	11. *finally*
2. *only*	7. *exactly*	12. *simply*
3. *actually*	8. *early*	13. *especially*
4. *probably*	9. *obviously*	14. *clearly*
5. *certainly*	10. *basically*	15. *quickly*

Adjectives
Although *–ly* usually indicates an adverb, this same two-letter ending can also be used to form a small number of adjectives from a noun (*day → daily; friendly → friendly*) or another adjective (*lone → lonely*).

Adjectives ending in *–ly* usually have one of two meanings:

Meaning	Examples
1. every (before nouns of time): *every hour → hourly* *every day → daily* *every month → monthly*	What is your *monthly* <u>salary</u>? The adjective *monthly* describes the noun *salary*.
2. acting like a _____ : *acting like a mother → motherly* *acting like a father → fatherly* *acting like a friend → friendly*	Leo is a very *friendly* <u>guy</u>. The adjective *friendly* describes the noun *guy*.

In the Corpus of Contemporary American English (COCA), 15 common *–ly* adjectives (in order of frequency) include:

1. *early*	6. *friendly*	11. *ugly*
2. *likely*	7. *weekly*	12. *deadly*
3. *daily*	8. *elderly*	13. *silly*
4. *holy*	9. *lovely*	14. *lonely*
5. *unlikely*	10. *monthly*	15. *costly*

Some *–ly* words can be an adjective or an adverb depending on the sentence: *I go for a <u>daily</u> run in the park* (adjective) or *I go for a run in the park <u>daily</u>* (adverb). Other examples include *early, nightly, hourly, weekly, yearly,* and *friendly*.

♦ Question 64 Doubling Final Consonants before Adding –ed or –ing

When we add a suffix like –ing, we double the final consonant (stop → stopped and bag → bagged), but what about the final letter is x? Which is correct: taxed or taxxed? Why?

When the final three letters of a word are **consonant-vowel-consonant (C-V-C)**, we double the last letter before adding a suffix such as –ed, –ing, –er, –est, –or. For example, the verb stop changes to stopping because the last three letters are t (consonant), o (vowel), and p (consonant), but the word meet does not change to *meetting because the last three letters are V-V-C: e (vowel), e (vowel), and t (consonant).

There are many words in English with vowel + –x, such as tax, fix, and box. Most letters represent only one sound, but the letter x actually represents two consonant sounds: /k/ and /s/. Therefore, for any word that ends in vowel + –x, the last three sounds are vowel-consonant-consonant (V-C-C), which means we do not double the final letter. Thus, the past tense of the verb fax is faxed: She faxed the pages to me.

While this simple explanation is clear, some teachers may wish to have a deeper understanding behind this spelling pattern. Another way to analyze when we double a final consonant is using the short vowels and long vowels. In general, we double the final consonant if that syllable has a short vowel sound. Therefore, we double the n in sin to sinned because the vowel sound is short i, but we do not double the n in sign to signned because the vowel sound is a long i. This is true, but the labels **short vowel** and **long vowel** are not useful to learners who did not go through elementary school in North America.

Most native speakers have never thought about why certain vowels sounds are called short and long when in fact one is not necessarily shorter than the other. For example, ran (short a) and rain (long a) are pretty similar in length, but back (short a) and bag (short a) are different in length. The short a in bag is actually longer than the short a in back. (The reason is that syllables that end in a **voiced sound** such as /g/ are held longer than those that end in a **voiceless sound** /k/.) Yes, the underlying reason for when to double a final consonant has to do with using a spelling pattern that will maintain short and long vowel pronunciations, but this is too much information for most English learners. In contrast, most learners know the difference between a consonant and a vowel and can therefore recognize C-V-C. Therefore, I recommend using the C-V-C approach to this lesson. Keep it simple! Don't make your learners learn two new concepts and labels (short vowel, long vowel) for a spelling rule that has a much easier option (C-V-C).

The letter *w* can be a consonant when it sounds like the *w* in *we*. However, when it occurs as the last letter in a word, it is silent, as in *view* or *follow*. Thus, the last sound is a vowel, and vowels are never doubled. No word in English ends with the letter *w* having a /w/ pronunciation, so the letter *w* is never doubled.

The letter *y* is a consonant when it sounds like the *y* in *yes*. However, when it occurs as the last letter in a word, it is silent (*play*), so the last sound is the vowel *a* before –*y*. Final vowels are never doubled because you need consonant-vowel-consonant. Since no word in English that ends with the letter *y* has a /y/ pronunciation, it is not doubled.

◆ **Question 65** *–er* vs. *–or: writer* vs. *author*

Writer is with –*er,* but *author* is with –*or*. Are there any rules for spelling a profession with –*er* or –*or*?

There are not any rules, but these are some general patterns:

1. verbs ending in –*ate* change to –*or*: *educate → educator, investigate → investigator*
2. verbs ending in a consonant + –*t* change to –*or*: *act → actor, invent → inventor*
3. –*er* is added to common verbs: *to drive → driver, to sing → singer*
4. –*er* endings are more common than –*or* endings
5. –*ist* endings are more common with more technical jobs, such as *dentist, scientist, hygienist, typist, hair stylist*

The suffixes *–er* and *–or* often share a meaning: a person or thing that does something. For example, a person who drives a taxi is a *taxi driver*, but a person who directs a movie is a *director*. *Driver* is spelled with *–er* and *director* is spelled with *–or*. Unfortunately, there are no solid rules about when to use *–er* and when to use *–or*, but the most common letter before *–or* is the letter *t*: *actor, doctor, visitor*.

The bottom line is that students need to learn the examples that are important for their English needs. Consider these common words:

Common Words Ending in *–er*		Common Words Ending in *–or*	
babysitter	player	actor	inspector
banker	police officer	author	inventor
builder	prisoner	calculator	investigator
cleaner	programmer	collector	janitor
computer	reader	conductor	operator
consumer	robber	creator	projector
customer	runner	director	professor
dishwasher	server	doctor	sailor
driver	singer	educator	supervisor
farmer	soldier	elevator	visitor
gardener	swimmer	governor	
lawyer	teacher		
leader	traveler		
manager	winner		
owner	worker		
photographer	writer		

In addition to *–er* and *–or*, this same meaning of "one who does" can also be spelled with *–ar* (*beggar*), *–ian* (*physician*), and *–ist* (*dentist*), but these three suffixes are less common.

This same pattern is also used with the meaning "a thing that does," so students also need to learn words that describe things such as *rice cooker* and *calculator*.

11 ◆ Verbs

Verbs are at the heart of every sentence. Making a mistake with a verb can seriously weaken people's perceptions of a student's English. Although the information in this chapter may seem overwhelming, it is all very important for students' success in English.

One of the most important components regarding verbs is the **verb tense**. For a more detailed account of verb tenses in English, see Chapter 2 and Keys 1–4 in Chapter 3 in *Keys to Teaching English to Language Learners, 2nd Edition* (Folse, 2016).

Three other important areas related to verbs are **auxiliary verbs**, **passive voice**, and **phrasal verbs**. These three are covered in Chapter 2 and Keys 2–4, 11, 12, 14, and 16 in Chapter 3 in *Keys to Teaching Grammar to English Language Learners, 2nd Edition* (Folse, 2016).

3 Common ESL Errors with Verbs

ESL Error	Explanation
1. *I live here since 2015.	Many ESL students struggle with the present perfect tense. While it has several meanings, one of the most common is for a past action that continues until now.
2. *At the start of the experiment, the temperature was measure at 78 degrees.	With passive voice, students sometimes do not use the correct form of the past participle.
3. *My brother no speak good English.	Negating in English is difficult. Sometimes learners forget that a verb that has only one word (*speak*) must use a form of the auxiliary verb *do* when negating the verb.

◆ Question 66 The Number of English Verb Tenses

How many verb tenses are there in English?

Every experienced ESL teacher should be able to list all of the verb tenses and provide an appropriate sentence context including key adverbs of time that we often associate with certain tenses. For example, simple past tense is used with *yesterday, last* _____, and _____ *ago.*

Verb Tense	Examples
simple present	He **works** at Lincoln Bank **every day.**
simple past	He **worked** at Lincoln Bank **last year.**
simple future	He **will work** at Lincoln Bank **next year.**
present progressive[1]	He **is working** at Lincoln Bank **now.**
past progressive	He **was working** at Lincoln Bank **when I met him.**
future progressive	He **will be working** at Lincoln Bank **at this time next year.**
present perfect	He **has worked** at Lincoln Bank **since 2015.**
past perfect	He **had worked** at Lincoln Bank **before he started here.**
future perfect	He **will have worked** at Lincoln Bank for twenty years **when he retires.**
present perfect progressive	He **has been working** at Lincoln Bank **since college.**
past perfect progressive	He **had been working** at Lincoln Bank **before I met him.**
future perfect progressive	He **will have been working** at Lincoln Bank for almost thirty years **when he retires next month.**

---

[1] In British English, the term *continuous* is used instead of *progressive.*

There are three divisions of time (present, past, future) and four **aspects** of each verb tense (simple, progressive, perfect, perfect progressive). Therefore, another way to visualize these 12 tenses is by listing the four aspects on one side of a grid and the three time elements across the top of the grid, producing the 12 tenses.

	Present	Past	Future
simple	works	worked	will work
progressive	is working	was working	will be working
perfect	have worked	had worked	will have worked
perfect progressive	have been working	had been working	will have been working

Teachers should note that many linguists say there are only two tenses (present and past) with multiple aspects. However, we are not training future linguists, so such theoretical musings, while potentially interesting, are of little practical value. Our students have ESL books to help them learn English, and all ESL books are based on the 12 verb tenses shown in this answer, so these are the 12 tenses that most ESL students learn.

◆ Question 67 The Most Frequent Verb Tenses in English

Which verb tenses are the most common in English? Which ones are the most important to study?

When someone asks about verb tenses, they are really asking about any kind of verb form that can appear after a subject. There are 12 verb tenses in English, but there are also two forms of **modals** (simple **modals**: *could go*; **perfect modal**: *could have gone*), and the **imperative** or **command** form (*Go there now!*). Therefore, there are 15 possible verb forms that could appear as the main verb in a sentence in English.

Verb Tense/Form	Example
simple present	You **go**
simple past	You **went**
simple future	You **will go**
present progressive	You **are going**
past progressive	You **were going**
future progressive	You **will be going**
present perfect	You **have gone**
past perfect	You **had gone**
future perfect	You **will have gone**
present perfect progressive	You **have been going**
past perfect progressive	You **had been going**
future perfect progressive	You **will have been going**
modal	You **should go**
perfect modal	You **should have gone**
imperative	**Go**

If we divide 100 by 15, we get 6.5 percent. Common sense tells us that each of these 15 verb forms is not used equally in writing or speaking—that is, 6.5 percent of the time. When was the last time you used future perfect progressive tense? Several of these tenses are rare, and a few occur much more frequently than others. In university student writing, three of the most common are simple present, simple past, and modals (Alzuhairy, 2016; Qahtani, 2017).

In a study of student writing assignments from an upper-level university English course, Alzuhairy (2016) examined 103,181 words and found that the most frequent forms were simple present (50 percent), simple past (29 percent), modals (10 percent), and present perfect (5 percent). The remaining 11 forms were used only 6 percent of the time, with 4 of those at less than 2 percent and 7 at 0 percent.

In a similar study, Qahtani (2017) examined 101,713 words of student writing from a university history course and found these results: simple past (44 percent), simple present (39 percent), and modals (9 percent). The remaining 11 forms were used 8 percent of the time, with 6 of those at less than 2 percent and 5 at 0 percent.

It is not the case that these other 11 verb forms are not important. However, for most students, it is really important to focus attention on simple present, simple past, modals, and present perfect.

◆ **Question 68 The Importance of the Verb** *be*

Why is the verb *be* so important in English?

The verb *be* (*am, is, are*) is usually the first verb students learn in English or any foreign language. The verb *be* is important in all languages that have *be*. Some languages like Arabic and Russian do not have *be* in present tense, although it exists in past tense. In Malay and Japanese, there is no *be* verb with subject + *be* + noun or subject + *be* + adjective.

In English, *be* is the most frequently used verb. In the Corpus of Contemporary American English (COCA), *be* is the most common verb. The eight forms of *be* (*be, am, is, are, was, were, been, being*) occurred 17,658,763 times (of 450 million words), so *be* is about 4 percent of the entire corpus. This means that a form of *be* appears once in every 25 words. Likewise, on the General Service List (West, 1956), *be* is the most frequently occurring verb and the second most common word overall on the list (just after *the*).

While some verbs tend to have only one or a very small number of functions in English, *be* has many usages, and that is why it is so important to know this verb well. Example usages include:

be as main verb	*be* + noun	She is a doctor.
	be + adjective	The weather is humid.
	be + prepositional phrase	The book is on the table.
	be + nationality	Juan is Mexican.
	be + age	Juan is 22 years old.
	be + adverb of place	The meeting will be here.
	be + adverb of time	My birthday was yesterday.
	be + noun clause	His answer was not what I expected.
be as helping verb (auxiliary verb)	*be* + verb + *-ing* (a progressive tense)	It is raining now.
	be + past participle (passive voice)	Arabic is written from right to left.

◆ Question 69 Negating Verbs

How do I make a negative sentence? Sometimes I put *not* (*I am not here*), sometimes *don't* (*I don't know*), and sometimes *didn't* (*I didn't go*). If I say *I don't have a car*, then why is it wrong to say **I don't have seen Maria*? Can you explain this?

The majority of negated verbs just add *not*. The ones that do not simply add *not* are in simple present, simple past, and command. Simple present uses *do not* and *does not* before the verb, while simple past uses *did not* before the verb. The command uses *do not*. In sum, sometimes we need to use the auxiliary verb *do* + *not* or *does* + *not* (for simple present tense) or *did* + *not* (for simple past tense), but there are many more times when we just use *not*.

A simple way to teach negating is that students should add *not* to verbs that have at least two words (*are eating, have been living, should go*). However, if a verb has only one word in the affirmative (simple present: *you work*, simple past: *you worked*, or command: *Eat!*), students must use the auxiliary verb *do* to help with negating.

The only exception is the verb *be* as a main verb. *You are here* has only one verb, but we do not need the auxiliary verb *do* before *not* because the main verb is *be* (*are*).

This student's question is about negating *I have seen Maria*. Because the verb *have seen* has two words, we simply add *not* after the first verb *have*. There is no reason to add *don't*.

At first glance, negating verbs in English appears to be difficult, and actually it is more complex than in many other languages. However, it really is simple after students see the clear patterns.

Consider the seemingly difficult case of the verb *have*, which can be a main verb and an auxiliary verb. In the sentence, *I have a car*, the verb is only one word (*have*), so English adds *do not: I do not have a car*. However, in the sentence, *I have eaten sushi*, the verb has two words already (*have eaten*), so English just adds *not* after the first one: *I have not eaten sushi*.

The word *no* is also used at the beginning of a response (*No, I don't understand*) or before a noun (*there is no milk in the refrigerator*). A common student error, especially at the beginning level, is to negate all verbs with the word *no*: **I no like tea, *My sister no speak English, *They no went to the bank*. This error is a normal, expected error made by speakers of many different native languages.

Verb Tense / Form	Verb	Affirmative	Negative
command	eat	Eat!	**Do not** eat!
simple present	be	you are	you are **not**
simple present	work	you work	you **do not** work
simple present	work	he works	he **does not** work
simple present	have	you have (a car)	you **do not** have (a car)
simple present	have	she has (a car)	she **does not** have (a car)
simple past	work	you worked	you **did not** work
simple past	have	you had (a car)	you **did not** have (a car)
simple future	need	you will need	you will **not** need
present progressive	live	you are living	you are **not** living
past progressive	live	you were living	you were **not** living
future progressive	live	you will be living	you will **not** be living
present perfect	make	you have made	you have **not** made
past perfect	go	you had gone	you had **not** gone
future perfect	eat	you will have eaten	you will **not** have eaten
present perfect progressive	live	you have been living	you have **not** been living
past perfect progressive	live	you had been living	you had **not** been living
future perfect progressive	live	you will have been living	you will **not** have been living
modal, *can*	speak	you can speak	you can**not** speak
modal, *might*	speak	you might speak	you might **not** speak
perfect modal, *must*	speak	you must have spoken	you must **not** have spoken
perfect modal, *should*	speak	you should have spoken	you should **not** have spoken

---

◆ **Question 70 Question Formation with *do***

Why it is wrong to say *What said the teacher to you?* My friend told me the correct question should be *What did the teacher say to you*? Why is *did* necessary here?

The real question here is, "How do you know when you need to use the form of *do* in a question?"

There are two basic ways to form a question in English. One is to invert the subject and the verb. The other way is to add a form of *do*, which can be *do, does,* or *did.*

If a **verb phrase** consists of two or more words, students should be taught to invert the first verb and the subject. Therefore, in the sentence *Joe has climbed Mt. Fuji three times*, the verb has two words (*has climbed*), so to form a question, put the first verb (*has*) in front of the subject, and that will result in this new sentence: *How many times has Joe climbed Mt. Fuji?*

If the verb has only one word (*said*), it cannot move to the beginning, so put *do, does,* or *did* in front of the subject to have two verbs in the question, one before the subject and one after the subject.

Question Word	*Do*	Subject	Verb	Rest of the Question
What	**did**	the teacher	say	to you?
Where	**do**	most people	purchase	their groceries?
Which bus	**does**	Emily	take	to her house?

A common error that ESL students make is omitting *do* (*do, does, did*) as in *What said the teacher to you?* The correct word order is this: Question word + *do* + subject + verb?

Notice that the helping verb *do* is not touching the main verb. In a question, the correct word order is to separate the auxiliary *do* (*do, does, did*) from the verb by putting the subject in the middle.

The only exception is the verb *be* as a main verb, which inverts even though it is only one word: *She is in Italy* becomes *Where is she?* Likewise, *The pilots were in France last year* becomes *When were the pilots in France?* We do not use the auxiliary *do* when *be* is the main verb.

Verb Tense / Form	Verb	Statement	Question
simple present	be	you are	Are you . . . ?
simple present	work	you work	**Do** you work . . . ?
simple present	work	he works	**Does** he work . . . ?
simple present	have	you have (a car)	**Do** you have (a car) . . . ?
simple present	have	she has (a car)	**Does** she have (a car) . . . ?
simple past	work	you worked	**Did** you work . . . ?
simple past	have	you had (a car)	**Did** you have . . . ?
simple future	need	you will need	Will you need . . . ?
present progressive	live	you are living	Are you living . . . ?
past progressive	live	you were living	Were you living . . . ?
future progressive	live	you will be living	Will you be living . . . ?
present perfect	make	you have made	Have you made . . . ?
past perfect	go	you had gone	Had you gone . . . ?
future perfect	eat	you will have eaten	Will you have eaten . . . ?
present perfect progressive	live	you have been living	Have you been living . . . ?
past perfect progressive	live	you had been living	Had you been living . . . ?
future perfect progressive	live	you will have been living	Will you have been living . . . ?
modal, *can*	speak	you can speak	Can you speak . . . ?
modal, *should*	speak	you should speak	Should you speak . . . ?
perfect modal, *should*	speak	you should have spoken	Should you have spoken . . .
perfect modal, *could*	speak	you could have spoken	Could you have spoken . . . ?

° ◆ **Question 71 Recognizing an Irregular Verb in the Past Tense**

Can you look at a verb and know whether it's regular or irregular in the past tense?

It is not possible to look at an unfamiliar verb and know whether it is regular or irregular in simple past tense.

A **regular verb** forms its past tense and past participle by adding –ed. The verb *need* is regular because the past tense is *needed*; the past participle is also *needed*. Likewise, the verb *want* is regular because its past tense is *wanted* and its past participle is *wanted*.

An **irregular verb** forms its past tense and past participle in several different ways, but, most obviously, these verbs do not add –ed (*see–saw–seen; write–wrote–written*).

10 Common Irregular Past Tense Verbs in Written English		
Verb	**Past Tense**	**Past Participle**
be (am, is, are)	was, were	been
do (do, does)	did	done
have (has, have)	had	had
say	said	said
make	made	made
go	went	gone
take	took	taken
come	came	come
see	saw	seen
know	knew	known

Data from Lancaster-Bergen Corpus.

One general guideline, however, is that an irregular verb is usually quite short. In fact, almost all irregular verbs are one syllable (e.g., *go, eat, see, take, fly*). There are only a few irregular verbs that have two syllables (e.g., *become*). Finally, a verb with three or more syllables is almost certainly a regular verb. For example, *multiply* (3 syllables), *investigate* (4 syllables), and *deteriorate* (5 syllables) are all regular verbs.

While many short verbs are irregular, students should not assume that all or even most short verbs are irregular. Sometimes a regular verb and an irregular verb can look very similar, but they form their past tense in very different ways. For example, the verbs *say* and *stay* look alike, but *say* is irregular and becomes *said*, but *stay* is regular and changes to *stayed*. Although the verbs *meet* and *greet* look alike, *meet* becomes *met* (irregular) and *greet* become *greeted* (regular), The verbs *set, let,* and *get* are very similar, but why do *set* and *let* remain the same in past tense, while *get* becomes *got*? If *need* becomes *needed*, why does *feed* become *fed*, not **feeded*?

20 Irregular Verbs with Higher Frequency in Past Tense		20 Irregular Verbs with Lower Frequency in Past Tense	
begin	put	bind	plead
come	read	breed	seek
do	say	cling	shine
drink	see	creep	slay
eat	speak	fight	slit
get	spend	flee	strike
give	take	forsake	undergo
go	tell	mislead	weave
have	think	overthrow	wind
make	write	partake	withstand

In conclusion, there is no way to accurately predict whether a one-syllable verb is regular or irregular in the past tense just by looking at it. As is the case with most foreign languages, learners have to memorize the irregular verbs. The good news is that irregular verbs impact one tense more than any other—simple past tense. In addition, the number of frequently used irregular verbs is perhaps 150, which is a quite a small number when you consider that English has thousands of verbs. No learner should ever be given a list of 150 items to memorize because not all of those items are necessary for that learner. Teachers should review a list of irregular verbs and decide which verbs are worth teaching based solely on whether or not their students will actually need them. With students at an intermediate and higher proficiency, another teaching technique is to ask the students to peruse a list of irregular verbs and let them choose the verbs they think they will need to use for their English needs. Some verbs are certainly more useful than others because students will need those verbs when they attempt to speak or write in English.

⬩ Question 72 Present Perfect Tense

What is the difference between _I worked_ at _Washington Bank_ and _I have worked_ at _Washington Bank_? Can I add the time phrase _in 2015_ to both of these?

These two verbs are different verb tenses. The verb _worked_ is in **simple past tense**, and the verb _have worked_ is in **present perfect tense**. These two tenses have very different meanings.

The verb _worked_ in simple past tense means it is finished. The verb _have worked_ might mean that the action is not finished, but it is not clear without more information. Most verb tenses have only one function, so logically past tense is for past and future tense is for future. However, present perfect tense is much more complicated because it has more than one function. Consider these four common usages:

Meaning	Examples
1. an action that began in the past but still continues now (past-to-present action)	I **have worked** at Washington Bank since 2010.
2. an action that took place in the past but the time is not mentioned; it is probably not happening now (indefinite past or unspecified time)	I **have worked** at Washington Bank.
3. an action that took place in the past (the time is not mentioned) that is relevant to the current situation (past-present connection)	_Ann:_ Do you think you have a good chance of getting that job at Lincoln Bank? _Sue:_ Well, yes, I do, because I **have worked** at Washington Bank, so I understand the job well.
4. a repeated past action	I **have worked** at three different banks.

It is possible to say *I worked at Washington Bank in 2015* because 2015 is finished, or in the past. Simple past tense can be used for actions with a specific past time such as *in 2015* (or *yesterday, last month, two weeks ago,* or *after I graduated from high school*).

Present perfect tense (*have worked*) is not possible with these time markers because it cannot be used with a specific past time such as *in 2015*. Instead, present perfect tense is used with less specific time markers such as *so far, ever, before, just,* or *many times*.

The present perfect tense is one of the most difficult tenses for English learners. On one hand, it is difficult because it has at least four different meanings. On the other hand, it is difficult because some languages, such as Arabic, Japanese, and Korean, do not have a similar form. In addition, other languages, such as French, have a very similar form that is used in a different way.

This tense is called **present perfect** because we use the present of the auxiliary verb *have* (*have* or *has*). It is called *perfect*, which means "completed" (from Latin) because the action was completed in relation to some other action or time. In *I have worked at National Bank since 2015,* we are comparing 2015 and now. In *She has written ten emails so far,* we are comparing when she started writing until now. In *Have you ever eaten sushi?* we are comparing your whole life with now.

Though this tense uses the word *present* in its name, it can be used for a wide range of times, which makes it even more difficult for learners:

- Present time (compared to past): *I have worked here since 2015.*
- Past time: *I have worked in Malaysia.* (I am not there now.)
- Future time: *After I have worked here for thirty years, I will retire.*

For more information about this difficult but important verb tense, see Chapter 2 and Keys 2 and 3 in Chapter 3 in *Keys to Teaching Grammar to English Language Learners, 2nd Edition* (Folse, 2016).

✦ Question 73 Progressive Tenses with Non-Action Verbs

Why is it wrong to say *These shoes are costing a lot of money,* but I can say *I am spending a lot of money*?

This question deals with why the verb *cost* is not possible in a progressive tense. *It is raining* and *I am eating* are possible, but not **I am having a car*, **They are needing a pencil*, or **These shoes are costing a lot of money*.

Which verbs are not very common in **progressive tenses**? In English, verbs that do not express a true action are not common in progressive tenses.

Examples of true **action verbs** are *read, write, run, play, stand, sit,* or *take*. These are verbs where someone is doing something. One way to think of these verbs is that these are verbs that someone could easily demonstrate the action or draw a picture of the action so that another person could guess the verb.

What are some **non-action verbs**? They often express a feeling (*like, want, need*), possession (*belong, have, own*), opinion or thinking (*believe, know, understand*), or a sense (*seem, appear, hear*).

Here are some verbs that are <u>not common</u> in progressive tenses:

believe	depend	hear	prefer	support
consist	hate	like	recognize	suppose
cost	have	love	smell	think

Sometimes a verb can be used in progressive but with a different meaning.

have	I *have* a book. ~~I am having a book.~~	no action, just possession; progressive is not possible
	I *have* a good time when I play tennis. I am playing tennis now, and I am *having* a good time.	action; progressive is possible

Language is always changing. For example, McDonald's used the phrase *I'm loving it* in 2003 to launch a new advertising campaign, and this phrase became very popular. Although we may see a few examples of non-action verbs in a progressive tense, such as in the McDonald's advertisement, it is still not very common in general English usage and tends to be limited to certain verbs.

◆ Question 74 *used to* before Verbs

I hear people say *I used to work there*. What does this mean? I know the verb *use*, but what is the connection between *used to* and the verb *use*?

The phrase *used to* before verbs is one of several ways to express past time in English. It has a very specific function in English that simple past tense (*I worked there*) or past progressive (*I was working there*) cannot provide. It is especially common in conversation.

The phrase *used to* refers to a repeated past action or habit that is no longer true. Therefore, *I used to work there* and *I worked there* may refer to the same general clock time of "before now," but they do not have the same nuance of meanings. *I worked there* tells only that this action was true at some point before now. Perhaps it was a single day, or perhaps it lasted twenty years. However, *I used to work there* tells us that it was much more than a single day, expresses possible repetition, and indicates that this action is no longer true and probably not going to happen again.

Some native speakers incorrectly think *used to* is slang or bad English, but that is not the case. The pattern *used to* + verb is a normal part of the English language. In fact, according to Online Etymology Dictionary (www.etymonline.com), the phrase *used to* has been common since around the year 1400, so it has a long history in English.

Used to originally came from the verb *use*, but today *used to* and *use* have two different meanings. They also have different pronunciations. The verb *use* in the past tense (*I used a pencil*) is pronounced with /z/ for the letter –*s* and /d/ for the final –*ed* sound. In contrast, the expression *used to* (+ verb) is pronounced with /s/ for the letter –*s* and /t/ for the final –*ed* sound.

It might be helpful to ask students to create and practice several personal and meaningful examples of something they no longer do: *When I was a child, I used to _____.* One answer might be *When I was a child, I used to hate onions.*

Your students may also know that it is possible to use *would* + verb instead of *used to* + verb for past repeated actions that no longer happen. However, we do not use *would* + verb for **stative verbs** such as *be, feel, hate,* or *love*. We can say *When I was a kid, I used to sleep late on Saturday mornings* or *When I was a kid, I would sleep late on Saturday mornings.* However, we can never say **When I was a kid, I would hate onions.*

♦ **Question 75** *be going to* vs. *will*

What is the correct way to talk about a future action? Do I use *be going to*? Or do I use *will*? Is there any difference?

In English, there are several ways to express a future action or event. Two common ways are *be going to* and *will*.

Most students have learned that the only way to talk about the future is through the modal verb *will*. However, that is not an accurate picture of how future is expressed in English. In fact, one of the main teaching points here is that students should not just use the word *will* to talk about the future.

Besides *will*, we also use *be going to* for an action in the future. In particular, we use this expression to talk about future actions or events that we have already planned. A verb with *be going to* usually takes the form: *be going to* + verb.

We also use *be going to* when there is strong evidence that something is going to happen. If the sky is full of very black clouds, you cannot say **Wow, it will rain*. In this case, you should say *Wow, it's going to rain.*

We also use *be going to* for actions that are about to happen very soon. If you and your friend want to cross the street at the corner, you might decide to start crossing. However, your friend could suddenly grab your arm and say *Wait! The light is going to turn green and then we can cross.*

One special use of *will* is for spontaneous decisions. The word *will* is used in spoken English to talk about future actions that we did not have a prior plan to do. For example, if someone is carrying a lot of books and cannot open the door, you might decide at that moment to help and say *I'll open the door for you.* In this case, *be going to* is impossible.

In addition, we use will to request that someone do something: *Will you help me with this work?*

Comparison of *be going to* and *will*		
Function	***be going to***	***will***
a planned future action	✔	
a future action based on strong evidence right now	✔	
an unplanned, spontaneous action		✔
a prediction	✔	✔

◆ Question 76 Modal Verbs

If you say *I need to go* and *We want to go*, what about *You should to go* and *They will to go*? Why are these last two not OK?

In general, the most common pattern for two consecutive verbs is verb + infinitive. That is why we say *need to go* (not **need go*) and *want to go* (not **want go*).

However, there is a small group of verbs called **modal verbs** that behave differently. Modals include *can, could, will, would, shall, should, may, might, must,* and *had better.* These modal verbs are always followed by the **simple form** or **base form**. It is called the simple or base form because it has no suffixes. It has no *–s*, no *–ed*, no *–ing*, and no *to*. If you look up any verb in the dictionary, it first lists the verb as *eat, and* never as *eats, eating, eaten,* or *ate.* It only says *eat,* so that is the simple or base form of the verb.

wrong: **You should to go to the library more so you can have a quiet place to study.*

wrong: **You should going to the library now.*

correct: *You should go to the library.*

Note that there are **phrasal modals** that require *to: be able to, have to, ought to, be supposed to.*

Modals are very common in both spoken and written English, so students need to be able to use modals correctly. In fact, in two studies (Alzuhairy, 2016; Qahtani, 2017) of native speaker writing by university students in English and history courses, modals were the third most frequent type of verb structure, after simple present tense and simple past tense. Because modals were more common than 10 of the 12 tenses, teachers should dedicate more instruction and practice time to modals than to less common tenses such as past perfect or future progressive.

◆ Question 77 *could* in Affirmative Statements

If I can say *When I was leaving home this morning, I couldn't find my keys*, why can't I say *When I was leaving home this morning, I could find my keys*? The first one is possible, but the second one is not. Why?

In English, *couldn't* describes when something was not possible, but the affirmative *could* cannot be used for an action that happened on just one single occasion. Instead, *was/were able to, managed to,* or the original verb in past tense should be used:

> Ann: Were you able to finish your report last night?
>
> ~~Bob: Yes, I could.~~
>
> Bob: Yes, I was able to.
> OR: Yes, I managed to finish it.
> OR: Yes, I finished it.

	Past General Ability (repeated)	Past Ability on One Occasion
affirmative	Sue <u>could read</u> well when she was 7 years old. Sue <u>was able to read</u> well when she was 7 years old.	~~When she arrived home, she could open the door.~~ When she arrived home, she <u>was able to open</u> the door. When she arrived home, she <u>opened</u> the door.
negative	Sue <u>couldn't read</u> well when she was 7 years old. Sue <u>wasn't able to read</u> well when she was 7 years old.	When she arrived home, she <u>couldn't open</u> the door. When she arrived home, she <u>wasn't able to open</u> the door.

◆ Question 78 Contractions with Short Affirmative Answers

When someone asks me *Will you go to class tomorrow?* why is it not OK to reply *Yes, I'll* instead of *Yes* or *Yes, I will?*

When answering a yes-no question, a long full answer or short answer is possible, but in conversation, it is much more common to give just a short answer.

For **yes-no questions**, an affirmative answer cannot end with a contraction. If I ask *Is today your birthday?* you can answer with a short answer *Yes, it is, No, it isn't,* or *No, it's not.* However, we cannot use just two words and say **Yes, it's.* Likewise, we cannot answer a question by saying **Yes, I'll, *Yes, I'm,* or **Yes, she's.*

Here are examples of some possible correct answers:

Question	Full Answer	Short Answer
Will you go tomorrow?	Yes, I'll go tomorrow. Yes, I will go tomorrow.	Yes, I will. I will. Yes.
	No, I will not go tomorrow. No, I won't go tomorrow.	No, I will not. No, I won't. No.
Is Robyn a teacher?	Yes, she is a teacher. Yes, she's a teacher.	Yes, she is. She is. Yes.
	No, she is not a teacher. No, she isn't a teacher.	No, she is not. No, she isn't. No.

This information applies to longer sentences as well. We cannot say **Marie isn't from Canada, but Stuart's* or **My sister hasn't flown across the Pacific, but I've.* Instead, we have to write out the last word. An affirmative statement of any length cannot end with a contraction.

◆ Question 79 Passive Voice

What is passive voice? How and when should I use it?

The **passive voice** is a grammatical structure that consists of the verb *be* and the **past participle**. The verb *be* should be in the correct tense to indicate the time of the action. In addition, it should also be singular or plural according to the **number** of the subject.

Examples of Passive Voice		
Subject	*be +* **Past Participle**	**Other Information**
This letter	was written	by George Washington.
Important medical research	is conducted	across the globe.
A cure for the common cold	may be discovered	in the near future.

For sentences in passive voice, the subject is the thing or person that receives the action of the verb. Therefore, it is important to understand that the subject is not doing the action.

In the first example, *This letter was written by George Washington,* the subject is *this letter.* Because *this letter* did not do the action (*write*), we use passive voice *was written.*

For sentences in **active voice**, the most important topic is the person or thing that is doing the action (the "doer" of the action). In these sentences, the subject is the doer of the action. The active equivalent for the first example is *George Washington wrote this letter.* The active verb is *wrote,* and the passive verb is *was written.*

In general, we use passive voice when we do not care or do not know who did the action. In *Important medical reserach is conducted across the globe,* we do not care who is doing the research; we care about *important medical reserach.* In passive voice, the subject of the sentence is the receiver of the action. The subject can be either a person or a thing.

In *Important medical reserach is conducted across the globe,* we could name the actors and add the phrase *by people: Important medical reserach is conducted by people across the globe.* However, the phrase *by people* does not tell us any new or important information and should be omitted.

To name the agent in a passive voice sentence, add *by* + **agent**: *The letter was written by George Washington*. However, in some cases, it sounds strange to name the agent. The agent is generally not named when it is not new information or when the agent is not important or just not known. Students should not write *Corn is grown in Iowa by farmers* because the agent (*farmers*) is obvious and unimportant.

Some sources claim that passive voice is not good and should be avoided in academic writing. This is simply not an accurate statement. In fact, passive voice occurs in both written and spoken language as well as in formal, planned language and informal, ordinary conversations. It is common in academic writing, particularly in certain disciplines. It occurs in reports (*The chemicals were combined in a special laboratory*), news (*Several cars were stolen*), and announcements (*A party is planned immediately after the game*). It is very common in regular conversations, too (*I don't think these cookies were baked long enough*). To write and speak English well, students need to know how to use passive voice. This means knowing both how to form it as well as when to use it.

◆ **Question 80 Phrasal Verbs**

Why do you say *turn on the light* with two words (*turn* and *on*)?

These two words (*turn on*) are called a **phrasal verb**. A phrasal verb consists of a verb followed by a **particle** such as *after, away, back, over, in, into, out, on, off, up,* or *down*. In the example *He didn't turn on the light*, the phrasal verb is *turn on*. Other common examples of phrasal verbs are *take up, pick out, call off,* and *make up*.

A particle looks like a preposition, but it is not a preposition. A **preposition** goes with a noun after it to form a unit called a **prepositional phrase**. In contrast, a particle goes with the verb to form a special meaning. It does not go with the noun object. In the example *He didn't turn on the light*, the word *on* is part of *turn on*, not part of *on the light*.

Consider the two sentences *She ran up the hill* and *She ran up the bill.* Each of these two sentences has three meaningful chunks or pieces.

Example	Analysis
1. She ran up the hill. (not a phrasal verb)	She + ran + up the hill. 1 2 3 S + V + PREP. PHRASE
2. She ran up the bill. (phrasal verb)	She + ran up + the bill. 1 2 3 S + V + D.O.

Only the second sentence has a phrasal verb. In the first sentence, the sentence can be divided into three parts: *She* (subject) + *ran* (verb) + *up the hill* (a prepositional phrase telling where she ran). The three parts of the second sentence are: *She* (subject) + *ran up* (a phrasal verb meaning "to increase"), and *the bill* (direct object).

Many English learners often avoid using phrasal verbs at first because they do not know about their existence and later because they appear to be more difficult. For every phrasal verb, there is almost always a single-word equivalent in English. These single-word equivalents are often of Latin origin and tend to be used in modern English in more technical or formal situations, while phrasal verbs are often of Anglo–Saxon origin (meaning they are from the original English before Latin and French words were introduced) and are very common in spoken English

For example, you might say *I turned down a job offer from that company,* but a formal report might say *We regret that you have rejected our generous job offer and hope you will reconsider.* If a child is sick, the doctor will ask, *Did you throw up?* but the bottle of medicine will say *Children: This medicine may cause some young children to vomit.*

Phrasal Verb	Latin equivalent
turn on	activate
take up	collect
pick out	select
call off	cancel
make up	invent, reconcile
run up	increase
put out	extinguish
throw up	vomit

Learners who speak Spanish, French, Portuguese, or Italian—which are languages from Latin—are much more likely to use a Latin-based word than a phrasal verb. However, not using phrasal verbs makes a student's English sound strange. A native speaker might say *I need to look into the price of a hotel room,* but an ESL student whose native language is from Latin (e.g., Spanish, French, Portuguese, Italian) would most likely say *I need to investigate the price of a hotel room.* This sounds strange because police do investigations, not tourists who are looking for a cheaper hotel room. The grammar of the sentence is not wrong, but this sentence is certainly not OK because the speaker wanted to sound natural in a regular conversation. Instead, a native speaker's ears would immediately be alerted to this unusual use of a formal word *investigate* in a friendly conversation. In this case, it is an error in **register**, not grammar. The language is just not appropriate for everyday, informal conversation.

For ESL students, phrasal verbs cause special problems in both grammar and vocabulary. To begin with, phrasal verbs are extremely common. They are used in both speaking and writing, and because they are verbs and verbs are so important, phrasal verbs often determine the meaning of an entire sentence or utterance. Consider the sentence *He should put _____ the shirt.* Notice how the meaning changes dramatically by adding *out, on, down, away,* or *back.* If he puts the shirt <u>on</u>, he is wearing it, but if he puts the shirt <u>away</u>, it is in the closet. The phrasal verb controls the meaning of the sentence.

Another confusing aspect is that there are two types of phrasal verbs: **separable** and **non-separable**. For separable phrasal verbs, the second part (the particle) can "float" when the object is a noun: <u>*write down*</u> *a number* OR <u>*write*</u> *a number* <u>*down*</u>. There is no difference in meaning or accuracy of these two interchangeable forms. However, when we change the words *a number* to a pronoun (*it*), we do not have the same two options. With a pronoun object, we have to separate the phrasal verb and say *write it down*, never **write down it*.

With non-separable phrasal verbs, the phrasal verb can never be separated, even with pronouns: *look after the baby* but not **look the baby after* or *look after her* but never **look her after*. Whether the object is a noun (*baby*) or a pronoun (*her*) does not matter with non-separable phrasal verbs.

Although phrasal verbs do present grammatical challenges, by far the most common ESL errors with phrasal verbs are lexical (i.e., vocabulary) mistakes, which indicate that learners need to focus more on the meaning of phrasal verbs. Phrasal verbs are usually idiomatic, which means that the meanings of the individual words do not add up to the meaning of the whole phrasal verb. How could a learner know that *take up* means to begin a new hobby, as in the sentence *I took up tennis in college*? The meanings of *take* and *up* in no way equal or even hint at this meaning of *take up*.

Further compounding the difficulty is the fact that most phrasal verbs are **polysemous**, meaning they have many meanings. For example, the phrasal verb *take up* has at least six different meanings.

Meanings of *Take Up*	
Definitions	**Examples**
1. begin a new activity	I **took up** tennis when I was 17 years old.
2. occupy space	I like this table, but it **takes up** a lot of space.
3. occupy time	Driving to and from work **takes up** several hours of my day.
4. accept an offer or invitation	I think I'll **take** you **up** on your offer to lend me your car this afternoon if that's still possible.
5. make something shorter	She asked the seamstress to **take up** her dress.
6. discuss at another time	Class, tomorrow we will **take up** how the War of 1812 began.

For a more in-depth discussion of phrasal verbs, see Key 11 in Chapter 3 in *Keys to Teaching Grammar to English Language Learners, 2ⁿᵈ Edition* (Folse, 2016) and the Introduction of *Vocabulary Myths: Applying Second Language Research to Classroom Teaching* (Folse, 2004).

◆ Question 81 Verb Tense with Certain Idioms

Why do we say *I've had it with Joe* when you are feeling frustrated with this person, but we can't say *I will have it with Joe* for the future or *I'm having it with Joe* right now?

The phrase *to have had it with someone* is an idiom. It means that you are not willing to work with or deal with that person any longer. For example, if your boss demands too much from you and you can no longer accept this type of treatment, you might say *I've had it with my boss!*

An **idiom** has a very limited meaning, and a few idioms also have grammar limitations. This idiom is one that has a very limited grammatical setting. In this case, the idiom *to have had it with someone* usually occurs in one of the three perfect tenses: present perfect tense (*have had it*), past perfect tense (*had had it*), or future perfect tense (*will have had it*). However, it occurs most often in present perfect tense.

Other examples of idioms that use limited verb tenses are *You're telling me* and *I'm all ears*. The idiom *You're telling me* means that the speaker already agrees with what the other person said. It is used only in present progressive tense. The idiom *I'm all ears* means that I am ready to listen. It can occur with several different tenses, but it is most frequently used in simple present tense.

> ◆ **Question 82 Limitations of Present Progressive Tense**
>
> If a child is misbehaving, we can say *he is being bad*. Why can't I also say *he is being hungry* or *he is being sleepy*?

There are some verbs that are rare in any progressive tense because they are not true actions. For example, if I think you are tired today, I cannot say **You are seeming tired* (present progressive tense) because the verb *seem* does not show an action the way a verb such as *play, eat,* or *dive* does. *Seem* is a **stative verb**, which means it describes a state or condition but does not show a true action (as most verbs do). Other stative verbs that are rarely in this tense include *belong, prefer, know,* and *be*. We don't say **this book is belonging to you, *she is preferring coffee, *I'm knowing the answer,* or **the car is being gray.*

However, some verbs can be both stative and action verbs depending on what they mean in a certain context. When *have* means "to possess," it is stative, so progressive is not possible. I can say *She had a car* (simple past tense), but not **She was having a car* (past progressive tense). When *have* means "to give birth," it is an action, so we can say *She had a baby* or *She was having a baby*. When *have* means "to experience," it is an action, so we can say *We have a good time when we are together* and *We are having a good time now.*

The verb *be* is similar. When *be* describes, it is a stative verb, not an action, so it cannot be in progressive tense. We can say *It is gray* but not **It is being gray*. We can say *It is cold* but not **It is being cold.*

When *be* means "to act" or "to behave," it implies some kind of action and can be used in a progressive tense.

The example of *he is being bad* means the child is crying, shouting, or running around right now. It means the child is doing something right now that explains the word *bad*, so it is possible to use with the present progressive tense.

The present progressive often implies a temporary situation (*I am living with my parents until I can find a job and move out*) while present tense implies a more permanent, longer situation (*I live with my parents*).

be	
Simple Present Tense	**Present Progressive Tense**
He is stubborn. (This is part of his general personality.)	He is being stubborn. (He is refusing to change his mind about something now. This sentence is about that stubborn action or actions. For example, someone apologized to him, and he will not accept the apology.)
She is rude. (She always does and says rude things.)	She is being rude. (She is doing something rude. This sentence is about that rude action. Perhaps she did not say *thank you* or maybe she just insulted someone.)

Many examples of *being* + adjective involve momentary personality behavior. In the example *he is being bad*, we can easily imagine many actions. In the example **he is being hungry*, it is difficult to imagine many actions to demonstrate hunger. In **he is being sleepy*, that is his mental state at that moment. When his eyes begin to close and his head drops, we can say *he is falling asleep* because that is the process to sleep, but there are not multiple actions that mean "be sleepy."

12 • Vocabulary Meets Grammar

For a long time, vocabulary did not get much attention in foreign language education. Teachers were told to concentrate on grammar because grammar was the heart of a language. The assumption was that knowing grammar well meant you then knew a language really well. At that time, the syllabus for any language course was heavily dominated by memorizing grammar rules. Unfortunately, knowing grammar rules did not necessarily enable anyone to speak that language well. In many countries, the emphasis on grammar has shifted somewhat to attention to vocabulary, which is a good thing because knowing vocabulary is what makes a person better able to express ideas in a new language. To be sure, grammar is important, but grammar is only the glue that holds all the vocabulary together. Without knowing lots of vocabulary, no one can function well in a new language.

Sometimes not knowing just one word can completely stop communication. In *Vocabulary Myths* (Folse, 2004), I recount several stories of my own studies of Japanese and Spanish in which not knowing one word had bad results. On just Day 3 of living in my new foreign country of Japan, not knowing the Japanese word for *flour* doomed my first grocery store interaction. Not only was I unable to buy the main ingredient for making biscuits, I had a pretty negative impression of my new host country because I ended up feeling very embarrassed as an adult trying to complete a normal-life transaction like grocery shopping. I knew basic Japanese grammar fairly well and could form sentences to express statements, questions, and negatives, so grammar was not the problem. However, grammar would not suffice. I needed to know more vocabulary. Likewise, not knowing the Spanish word *comida* in the phrase *sin comida* gave my Nicaraguan friends a good laugh when I interrupted their Spanish conversation to ask about the phrase *cinco mida*, which I thought I had clearly heard. Despite their laughter, I kept insisting that one of my friends had mentioned **five midas*. The only problem with this is there is no word *mida* in Spanish. Most people who have attempted a foreign language can usually remember one or more times when limited vocabulary, not grammar, caused a communication problem.

One of the most difficult challenges for all foreign language teachers is helping our students realize that learning a new language requires much more than translating word for word. In fact, one clear sign of an unsuccessful language learner is that person's inability to accept the fact that languages do not have a word-to-word correspondence. Just because it takes four words to say *I'm 25 years old* in English does not mean that every language needs four words to express the same idea.

3 Common ESL Errors with Vocabulary Meets Grammar

ESL Error	Explanation
1. *For my master's degree, I made research about English speakers who are learning Chinese.	Many languages have only one word that means both *do* and *make*, which causes confusion for English learners. Expressions that use *do* and those that use *make* must be memorized. In English, we *do* research.
2. *She said me what happened.	Unlike English, many languages (e.g., Spanish, French, Japanese) have one word that means *say* and *tell*, so confusion and errors are inevitable. In English, the verb *say* is not followed by an indirect object. If we want to include *me* here, we have to use *tell*: *She told me what happened.*
3. *How much people are in your group?	For many English learners, *many* and *much* look alike and have the same meaning. However, the two are very different in English. We use *many* with count nouns such as *people* and *much* with non-count nouns such as *money*.

◆ Question 83 *be* vs. *have*

In my language, we say *I have hungry*. In English, why is it
I am hungry?

Regardless of your students' native language, it is likely they will
make errors with *be* and *have*. This confusion is natural for beginning students in particular.

Speakers of languages such as Spanish, French, Portuguese,
Italian, German, and others use *have hunger* instead of *be hungry* as
we do in English. Thus, it is logical that some beginning students
might translate word for word and mistakenly say **I have hungry*.

Here is a useful chart with several *be* + adjective phrases in
which some ESL students might incorrectly use *have* due to first
language interference. This chart, or an adaptation, could be put up
in the classroom as the week's **word wall**.

be + Adjective Phrase	Examples
be hungry	I'm hungry. Are you hungry?
be thirsty	Are you thirsty?
be _____ years old	How old are you? I am 12 years old.
be right	I think Maria is right in this case.
be lucky	If you're lucky, you might win the prize.
be hot	I'm hot. Can you open a window?
be cold	Are you cold?
be sleepy	I'm so sleepy.
be afraid	We were afraid we would miss our flight.
be careful	Be careful with that knife!

Even students whose native language does not use *have* in these
expressions may make errors by confusing the two. For instance, all
beginning-level students are bombarded with *I am, you are, he is,
she is* and at the same time *I have, you have, he has, she has,* so it is
logical that they might start to confuse the two. In addition, speakers of Arabic are at a disadvantage because there is no verb *to have*
and there is no verb *to be* in present tense in Arabic. Thus, Arabic
speakers may confuse the two verbs with the option of no verb:
Maria is afraid, *Maria has afraid, *Maria afraid.

English has thousands of adjectives, but the good news is that the number of adjectives that students tend to misuse with *have* is relatively small, certainly not more than twenty. Useful teaching techniques include:

1. Helping students become aware of ten common adjectives that are often mistakenly used with *have* (as in the *be* + adjective phrase chart).

2. Creating a word wall with correct and incorrect example sentences.

3. Asking students to do exercises where they are forced to choose between *be* or *have*: *Maria (has, is) hungry now; Maybe the baby (has, is) cold; Sometimes the rain (has, is) heavy*; or, in the case of Arabic, three choices—*Maria (has cold, is cold, cold)*. (Be sure to include some sentences with *has* and some with *is* as the correct answer.)

4. Asking students to complete error identification exercises in which they are required to identify the error, explain how to correct it, and perhaps offer a reason students might make this particular error: *Maria has hungry now; There has 3 cats near the door; I have a car new.* (Include a few other types of errors in grammar they have been taught so that *be* or *have* is not the obvious target every time.)

◆ **Question 84** *a few* vs. *a little*

What is the difference between *a few* and *a little*?

In English, there are two phrases that can refer to a small quantity of something: *a few* and *a little*. Both of these phrases are similar in meaning, but the difference is in the type of noun that comes after each. *A few* is used with **count nouns**, and *a little* is used with **non-count nouns.**

We use *a few* before nouns that we can count. This noun is always plural. For example, we say *a few books* because we can count books. We can say *one book, two books, three books.* For the same reason, we say *a few days, a few sandwiches, a few reasons,* and *a few people.* It is never OK to say **a little days* or **a little sandwiches.*

We use *a little* before nouns that we cannot count. For example, we say *a little rice* because we cannot count rice. We cannot say **one rice, *two rices, *three rices.* For this reason, we say *a little money, a little information, a little sugar.* It is never OK to say **a few money* or **a few information.*

	Count	Non-Count
a small quantity	a few books	a little information

It is possible to use *a little* in front of a singular count noun, but the meaning is different. In this case, it refers to the size of that noun. For example, you can say *a little book*, but this means the book is small.

What is the difference between *many, much,* and *a lot of*?

In English, there are three similar ways to refer to a large quantity of something: *many, much,* and *a lot of.* These phrases are similar in meaning, but the grammar difference is in the noun that comes after them. *Many* is used with plural **count nouns**, and *much* is used with **non-count nouns**. *A lot of* can be used with all nouns.

We use *many* before nouns that we can count. For example, we say *many books* because we can count books. We can say *one book, two books, three books.* For the same reason, we say *many days, many sandwiches, many reasons,* and *many people.* It is never OK to say **much days* or **much sandwiches.*

We use *much* before nouns that we cannot count. For example, we say *much rice* because we cannot count rice. We cannot say **one rice, *two rices, *three rices.* For this reason, we say *much money, much information.* It is never OK to say **many money* or **many information.*

The phrase *a lot of* can be used with both count and non-count nouns. In other words, it can be used with all nouns. It is important to remember, however, that *a lot of* is not formal English and should not be used in academic writing. In conversation, it is extremely common.

	Count	**Non-Count**
a large quantity	many books a lot of books	much information a lot of information

One additional point is that *much* is not common in affirmative statements. It occurs more often in negative statements and in questions. For example, we can say *I don't have much money,* but it is not OK to say **I have much money.*

A related and very common learner error is to pluralize non-count nouns: **advices, *homeworks, *informations, *researches.*

♦ **Question 86** *make* vs. *do*

Make and *do* confuse me. In my language, we have one word for these two. When should I use *make* and when should I use *do*?

We use *make* or *do* depending on the other words that follow them. For example, *we make the bed*, but *we do the dishes*. There is no special reason; these are idiomatic usages.

In general, we use *make* to indicate creating or producing something new. We say *make breakfast, make a report,* and *make a plan.* In general, we use *do* with different kinds of work. We say *do a job, do work,* and *do homework.*

These expressions are idiomatic and must be memorized.

Special Expressions with *Make*		Special Expressions with *Do*	
make the bed	make a mistake	do work	do business
make dinner	make a promise	do the laundry	do badly
make money	make a decision	do homework	do well
make a living	make an excuse	do it over	do housework
make a difference	make a report	do a favor	do the ironing
	make a movie	do a job	do the dishes
make an agreement	make a suggestion	do research	do an exercise
		do a study	do exercise
		How do you do?	do an assignment
		What do you do?	How are you doing?

Longer lists of examples of *make* and *do* can be found in almost any grammar book or on the internet, but long lists can be overwhelming. When you find a good list, a useful technique to use with your students is to ask them to go through the list to see how many of the items they already know. This helps students see that the list is not all new information, which can reduce their anxiety and learning load.

Another useful technique is to ask students to look at the list of items and select the ten items that they think they will need to use in their English. On this list, for example, a person who is studying business or who will use English for business purposes might select expressions such as *make a plan, do business, make progress,* and *make an agreement.* In this way, students can have more control over their own learning as they focus on their actual language needs.

◆ **Question 87** *say vs. tell*

What is the difference between *say* and *tell*? The meanings seem similar to me, so why is it wrong to ask *What did he say you?*

The basic meanings of *say* and *tell* are very similar, if not the same. In fact, sometimes one dictionary defines *tell* by using *say* and then defines *say* by using *tell*. In many languages, there is only one word that means *say* and *tell*. For instance, the Spanish verb *decir* can be *say* or *tell* depending on the surrounding words in the context.

The real difference between *say* and *tell* is with the **syntax,** or grammar, of the two words.

Rule or Pattern	Example

After *say*, we put the speaker's message (direct object). The message (direct object) may be a noun or a noun clause.	He said <u>hello</u>. (noun)
	      D.O.
	He said <u>he was hungry</u>. (noun clause)
	      D.O.

If we have a <u>quote</u>, we usually use *say*, not *tell*.	He said, "I'm hungry."

After *tell*, we usually identify the listener (indirect object) just before the speaker's message (direct object).	He told <u>me</u> <u>the news</u>. (noun)
	    I.O. D.O.
	He told <u>me</u> <u>he was hungry</u>. (noun clause)
	    I.O. D.O.

When the direct object is a noun clause, the word *that* is optional.	He told me he was hungry. He told me (that) he was hungry.
It is also possible to omit the message.	Yes, he told me.
When reporting someone's command with *say*, we use *say* + infinitive. We do not identify the listener.	The boss said to finish these files by 8 PM.
When reporting someone's command with *tell*, we use *tell* + *listener* + infinitive. We identify the listener.	The boss told us to finish the files by 8 PM.

S - AV

IO - DO

In addition to the syntactic differences, there are some expressions that use only *say* or *tell*.

Expressions with *Say*	Expressions with *Tell*
say yes	tell a joke
say no	tell a story
say hello	tell the truth
say good-bye	tell a lie
say good morning	tell the time
say good afternoon	tell me why/how/when/where
say good night	tell the difference between A and B
say something	tell A and B apart
say nothing	tell a secret
say anything	don't tell anyone
say thanks	
say please	
say it out loud	
say what you want to say	

There are also idioms that use either *say* or *tell*.

Say	*Tell*
It goes without saying. (It is not necessary to say something because it is obvious.)	*You can never tell.* (Some things are just too difficult to know beforehand.)
That is easier said than done. (Doing something is more difficult than talking about doing it.)	*Tell me about it.* (I agree with you.)
You can say that again! (I completely agree with you.)	*You're telling me!* (I agree with you, so you do not need to tell me.)
Say cheese! (Smile! This is what a person says before taking a picture.)	*What did I tell you?* (I was right.)

Teachers should always focus on learner needs, so any good lesson would start with your learners' challenges. For example, one of the main errors that ESL learners make is using an object pronoun after the verb *say*: *Say me your name*; *He said me the address*; *Say me what you are thinking*; *He said me to call his mother*. All of these examples should use *tell* because they are followed by an indirect object, *me*. An easy point to tell your students is to memorize "Say X" and "Tell me X." There are other patterns, but these are two very common patterns that students should learn for *say* and *tell*.

◆ **Question 88** *other, another, the other*

Why is it wrong to say *Wow, these cookies are great! Please give me other cookie*?

The meaning of *other*, as well as *another* and *others*, is "additional." All three words have the same basic meaning, but they do not have the same grammar.

To talk about one thing that is not specific, we use *another*. The sentence *I need other book* is not correct. *Book* is a singular **count noun**, and there is a rule in English that a singular count noun must have the articles *a, an,* or *the*—or some other **determiner** such as *my, your, his, her, this, that, one*—in front of it. The bottom line is that *other* cannot be used all by itself with a singular count noun.

To check this sentence, take out the word *other* and look at what remains: *Please give me cookie*. This is not good English because we have to say *Please give me a cookie*. Now, if you take this last sentence *Please give me cookie* and put in the word *other*, you get *Please give me other cookie*, which is not right because the article *a* is needed. However, if *a* is added, *Please give me a other cookie* is the result. The problem is that *other* begins with a vowel sound, so we need *an*, not *a*, which produces *Please give me an other cookie*.

This used to be correct, but over time, English has come to write *an + other* in one word: *another.* The correct sentence should be: *Please give me another cookie.*

It is also possible to use *other* with a determiners such as *the, this, that, my, your,* etc.: *Where is the other car? My other brother lives in Chicago.*

Other can be used with singular (*Where is your other brother?*) or plural (*Tell me about your other brothers*).

The word *others* is a pronoun and cannot appear before a noun: *Some people ride a bus to the office, but others prefer to go by car.* In the second clause, the word *others* is a pronoun functioning as the subject. It is not possible to add a noun immediately after it: **others people* or **others students.*

Learners at all levels have persistent problems with the forms of *other.* Teachers should teach the usages of *other* that are most frequent and therefore potentially of most value to their learners.

◆ **Question 89** *too* vs. *very*

When I wrote *In my country, the desert is too big,* my teacher circled *too* and wrote *very* above it. Why? Is *too* wrong? What is the problem with *too*? I thought *too* is like *very,* but stronger.

To understand what the error is here means considering the **semantics** and grammar of the word *too.* Semantically, the student may think that *too* is stronger than *very.* In other words, this student might mistakenly believe that *too* means "very very," which is not the case. Grammatically, *too* and *very* are both adverbs of degree, and both are intensifiers. However, in terms of semantics, the meanings of these two words are not the same.

If this student means the desert in his country is not small, he should say *In my country, the desert is very/really/extremely big.*

The **intensifier** *too* has a special meaning of "more than enough," but it is a negative idea. We use the word *too* with the meaning of *very* before an adjective or adverb only when we intend a negative connotation, which in turn often implies (or directly means) that something else is not possible. For example, in the sentence *the desert is too big* the student would have to continue with more information: *In my country, the desert is too big for anyone to cross in one day.*

These examples, though possible in English, are most likely unintended errors if spoken by beginning ESL learners.

Error	Possible Correction
*This book is too interesting	This book is very interesting.
Everyone likes Susan. *She is too nice.	She is so nice.
*This sandwich is too delicious.	This sandwich is really delicious.
*I have too many books.	I have a lot of books.

Native speakers might say *Susan is too nice,* but it means that we think that she allows people to take advantage of her and therefore we think she should not be so nice to everyone. However, this kind of information should probably not be explained to ESL students because this was most likely not their intended message and would therefore be confusing to most students. The student who wrote this sentence probably really believed that *too* means "very very," which is most definitely not correct.

In these correct examples of *too,* notice the negative connotation of the adjectives:

Sentence	Negative Meaning
Amy: Are you flying to Paris in first class? Bob: It is too expensive.	Bob is telling Amy why it is not possible for him to fly in first class.
Tim: I studied Chinese, but it was too hard.	Tim could not learn Chinese.
Kim: Wait! Those potatoes are too hot to eat right now.	It is not possible to eat the potatoes right now.

In general, *too* tends to go with adjectives and adverbs that have a negative meaning (*expensive, hard, hot*). Adverbs such as *very, so, really,* and *extremely* can go with positive and negative words.

Example	Possible Meaning
This cake is really sweet.	This cake is sweet, and I like it.
This cake is really dry.	This cake is dry, and I don't like it.

Teachers should tell students that *too* is not a stronger form of *very*. Although they have grammatical similarities (e.g., they are both adverbs that intensify and they both go in front of an adjective or adverb), they have different meanings. Perhaps the best teaching strategy, especially with lower-proficiency students, is to tell them it is not common to use *too* with positive adjectives.

◆ **Question 90** *for* vs. *since*

What is the difference between *for* and *since* when we are talking about time?

Show students these two sentences:

Jill has worked here **since** 2010.

Jill has worked here **for** three years.

We use *since* with a specific day, date, time, or event: *since 2010, since Monday, since 9:30, since noon,* or *since this store first opened.* These time expressions all answer the question *when?* They tell when an action began.

In contrast, we use *for* with a period of time: *for three years, for two days, for an hour,* or *for most of my life.* These phrases all answer the question *how long?* They tell the duration of an action.

The word *since* can be a **preposition** or a **conjunction**. The word *for* is usually a preposition.

When *since* is a preposition, it can be followed by a noun. In this example, *2010* is the object of the preposition *since*:

Jill has worked here since 2010.

preposition + object

When *since* is a conjunction, it introduces a clause (subject + verb):

Jill has worked here since this store first opened.

conjunction + clause (S + V)

In this example, *the store first opened* is a clause following the conjunction *since*. In this clause, *store* is the subject and *opened* is the verb.

With this same meaning, *for* is a preposition. It is followed by a noun (or pronoun):

• Jill has worked here for three years.

preposition + object

In this example, *years* is the object of the preposition *for*.

Both of these prepositions have the same general meaning, but one emphasizes the start of the time period (*since*), while the other emphasizes the duration of the time period (*for*). If you want to emphasize when the action began, use *since*. If you want to focus more on the duration, then use *for*.

One short-cut for your students to remember when to use *for* or *since* is that *for* is often used with nouns ending in –*s*: *for two years, for three weeks*. Of course *for* can also be used for the singular forms of the same time words: *for one year, for a week*.

◆ **Question 91** *maybe* vs. *may be*

What is the difference between *maybe* and *may be*?

The word *maybe* is an adverb. It has the same meaning as *perhaps*. The usual place for *maybe* is at the beginning of a sentence (*Maybe it's going to rain again tomorrow*).

The phrase *may be* is a combination of the **modal** verb *may* and the verb *be*. The modal *may* can go with any verb in English, so we can say *he <u>may</u> go there, he <u>may</u> work there,* or *he <u>may</u> be there.* The usual place for *may* (or any modal) is after the subject and in front of the verb, which in this case is *be*.

maybe	**Maybe** the teacher will postpone the test if we all ask him.
	Maybe the cost of oil was not so high in 1980. Do you recall?
	Maybe she didn't really understand what you had said.
may be	I can't read that word. It **may be** *kilo* or it may be *kale*.
	Unfortunately, your wallet **may be** in the washing machine.
	In the future, the price of gasoline **may be** under a dollar a gallon.

> ◆ **Question 92** *because* vs. *because of*

> When do I use *because* and when do I have to use *because of*? What is the difference?

Show students these two examples:

> **Because** the weather was bad, my flight was canceled.

> **Because of** the bad weather, my flight was canceled.

Both *because* and *because of* express the same idea, so there is no vocabulary difference. They both explain the reason for something.

The difference is grammar. The word *because* is a **conjunction**, so it is followed by a **clause** (a subject and a verb). In contrast, *because of* is a **preposition**, so it is followed by a **noun** (or pronoun) or **noun phrase**.

If the reason is a clause, we use *because*. If the reason is a noun, we use *because of*.

In the first example, the reason is *the weather is bad*, which is a clause, so the speaker uses the conjunction *because*. In that clause, *weather* is the subject and *was* is the verb:

> Because the <u>weather</u> <u>was</u> bad, my flight was canceled.

> conjunction + clause (S + V)

In the second example, the reason is *weather*, which is a noun, so the speaker uses the preposition *because of*. In the prepositional phrase *because of the bad weather*, the noun *weather* is the object of the preposition *because of*:

> Because of the bad <u>weather</u>, my flight was canceled.

> preposition   +   object

In a search of the Corpus of Contemporary American English (COCA), the conjunction *because* occurred 11,600 times, but the preposition *because of* appeared only 4,700 times (as of the writing of this book). Thus, *because* is 2.14 times more common than *because of*. This corpus data shows us that *because* is much more frequent than the preposition *because of*. Students should learn not only the correct grammatical usage but also the relative frequency of actual usage. *Because of* may sound more formal or more academic and is therefore not to be used so frequently in everyday conversation.

I hear the word *so* all the time. What does it mean? How can I use it if I want to improve my English?

The word *so* is **polysemous**. Some dictionaries list more than 20 meanings for *so*, but no ESL student needs to know 20 meanings of any word. Here, we will only focus on seven common and useful meanings in English. Each has a different syntax (grammar) and sometimes a different punctuation.

The more common a word is, the more polysemous it is. A word is common not so much because of its single, core meaning but rather because that word is actually used in more than one sense. For example, the word *take* is polysemous. If you take a job, you "accept" that job offer, but *take* has a much higher frequency in English than *accept* because you also *take a shower, take your time, take a bus, take a pill*, and *take a walk*, none of which is connected to the meaning of "accept."

When students ask for the meaning of a word, they do not expect the teacher to be a dictionary and give all of the possible meanings. If students want all the meanings, then can and will consult a dictionary. Many students ask a teacher about the word when they really want the teacher to tell them what the most important meanings are. In essence, they are asking the teacher to give the single most important meaning that the students should know or they want the teacher to give a list of two or three possible meanings that are worth knowing.

Learner needs are always paramount, so teachers should focus on the meanings of *so* that are most beneficial for their students. For example, if it is a conversation class, then the use of *so* instead of *very* should be high on the list (*I was so hungry*). If it is an academic writing class, this same meaning would not be taught because *very* and other adverbs are probably more appropriate for academic writing. In a writing class, the teacher would certainly cover the use of *so* as a **coordinating conjunction** where *so* gives a reason or introduces a purpose (*The roads were icy, so people avoided driving.*). No one knows any learners' needs better than the teacher, so it is up to teachers to make these decisions.

Meanings of *so*	Example	Notes
very	It was <u>so</u> hot.	In conversation, *so* is often used in place of *very*, which is a surprisingly rare word in normal conversation.
result	It was hot, <u>so</u> we went swimming.	When *so* is a coordinating conjunction meaning a result, you have to use a comma to separate the two clauses.
reason or purpose	We went swimming <u>so</u> [that] we could cool off.	When *so* introduces the reason for something, you can put the word *that* or omit it. In either case, no comma is needed or possible.
also	I went swimming, and <u>so</u> did Tim.	The phrase *and so* is the same as *and . . . too*. (I went swimming, *and Tim did, too*.)
true, yes	Yes, I think <u>so</u>.	Common verbs in this pattern are *think, believe,* and *hope*.
continuing a conversation	Joe: I'm tired of this job. Ann: <u>So</u>, have you been looking for another?	In normal conversations, it has become very common for sentences to begin with *so*. It is a way of connecting people's ideas.
Why does it matter?	<u>So</u>?	In informal spoken English, *so* means "What is the big deal?" It implies that what was just said does not matter.

◆ **Question 94 Meanings of** *like*

I hear my American friends say the word *like* all the time, but it's not when they like coffee or they like football. For example, what does *I think classes start like August 25th* mean? What are the different meanings of the word *like*?

The word *like* has multiple meanings. Each of these is a different **part of speech**, so each does a different job in a sentence.

Part of Speech	Examples
verb	I like coffee, but I don't like tea.
preposition	A tricycle is like a bicycle.
conjunction	The final report should be ten pages like the professor said.
noun	Everyone has likes and dislikes.
adverb	"The food was, like, spicy."
adjective	They share like opinions.
interjection	"And then she said, like, she was so tired of school."

The most common meaning of *like* is as a verb. It is the meaning that many students probably learn early in their English studies.

Another common usage for the word *like* is as a preposition that means "similar to." When *like* is a preposition, it is always followed by a noun (or pronoun). In the sentence *A tricycle is like a bicycle*, *like* is a preposition and *like a bicycle* is a prepositional phrase.

Until relatively recently, the use of *like* as a conjunction (i.e., when it is followed by a subject and a verb) was considered incorrect English. Although today it is generally considered OK to say *Like I was telling you*, until only a very few decades ago, *like* was never acceptable as a conjunction.[1] Instead, only *as* was used in this case: *As I was telling you.*

Since the advent of Facebook and other forms of social media, *like* has a new noun meaning, which can be singular or plural, as in "Hey, my pic at Disney in Orlando got a *like* from my Aunt Mary."

---

[1] For more information on this controversy, do an internet search of "*like* as controversy." Specifically, search for information about the 1954 advertising campaign for Winston cigarettes.

As an interjection, there is a slang use of the word *like* that is considered very informal spoken English. It is the use of *like* as a filler word or interjection, as in *I was, like, so tired, and so, I told the hotel clerk, 'Like, I need a room. Like, right now because I'm so tired.'* This usage is not considered standard English, and it should never be written in any serious writing. Some students may try to copy this in their speech to fit in better with others around them, but they need to know when it is OK to talk this way and when it is not OK to talk this way. The social context is important.

In addition, there are two common conversation questions that perplex ESL students, so these deserve special attention in ESL classrooms. These questions are: *What does _____ look like? What is _____ like?*

The question *What does Matt look like?* is confusing with the verb *like* because *like* is not a verb in this question. The verb is *look*. This question is also confusing because the answer typically would not use the wording in the question. No one answers, for example, *Matt looks like a young man*. Instead, they describe Matt physically, as in *Matt is tall with blond hair.*

What is Matt like? sounds only slightly different from *What does Matt like?* Take a minute to say the pair out loud one after the other but in normal speed: *What's Matt like? What does Matt like?* Can you hear how similar they sound, especially to an ESL learner who expects *like* to mean the core meaning of *like*, as in *I like coffee?* A possible answer to the question *What is Matt like?* would be *He's a very nice guy.*

ESL learners need to be taught three questions that use the word *like* and the possible responses to those questions: *What does Matt like?* (He likes coffee.) *What does Matt look like?* (He has dark hair and green eyes.) *What is Matt like?* (He's smart and kind of quiet.)

◆ **Question 95** *never* vs. *ever*

What's the difference between *never* and *ever*? Are they opposites?

The word *never* has a very clear meaning "not at any time." When you say *President Kennedy never visited China,* it means that he did not go to China during his entire life.

The word *ever* is more complicated. *Ever* means "at any time." *Ever* is used in questions, comparatives, superlatives, and in negative statements.

Meaning	Examples
at any time	Have you <u>ever</u> eaten sushi? (question)
	The weather is warmer than it has <u>ever</u> been. (comparative)
	This is the best shrimp salad that I've <u>ever</u> eaten. (superlative)
	My cat hardly <u>ever</u> eats fish. (negative)

Here are some common student errors:

Student Error	Possible Corrections
*I have ever gone to my grandparents' house.	I go to my grandparents' house all the time.
	I have gone to my grandparents' house many times.
Bob: Have you ever eaten sushi? Ann: *Yes, ever.	Ann: Yes, a few times.
	Ann: No, never.

These errors occur because students mistakenly believe that *never* is the opposite of *ever,* so if *never* means "0% of the time," then *ever* must mean "100% of the time, or always."

◆ **Question 96** *used to work* vs. *be used to working*

What's the difference between *She used to work there* and *She's used to working there*?

Although these two sentences look very similar, their meanings are very different.

Pattern	Example	Meaning
used to + verb	I *used to* wake up at 6 AM.	In the past, I woke up at 6 AM. It happened multiple times. It occurred over a long period of time. I do not wake up at 6 AM now.
be + *used to* + verb + *-ing*	I'm *used to* waking up at 6 AM.	I wake up at 6 AM every day. This is a current situation. I may not like it, or it may be difficult, but I am accustomed to doing this action now.

The pattern *used to* + verb is for a repeated past action that is no longer true and probably not going to happen again.

In the pattern *be* + *used to* + verb + *–ing,* the word *used* means "accustomed." This pattern describes an action you do now that is part of your routine. You do it, you may not like doing it now, and you're likely to continue doing it.

While *used to* is followed by a verb (*I used to hate onions*), the expression *be used to* is followed by a noun. When the noun is an action, we use the *–ing* form, or gerund (*I am used to eating a late dinner*). We can also use a noun that is not a gerund (*I am used to the hot weather here in Florida*).

◆ **Question 97** *shall* vs. *will*

When do you use *shall*?

Shall is rare in modern American English. In the Corpus of Contemporary American English (COCA), *will* is 55 times more common than *shall* (as of the writing of this book). There are 1,037,222 examples of *will* but only 18,752 usages of *shall*. This shows the huge difference in current usage of *shall* and *will*.

One possible use of the modal verb *shall* is to make a suggestion or offer or to get advice by asking a question. Common questions include *Shall we go now?* (suggestion) and *Shall I sit here?* (make a request). In these examples, however, most people today would probably use *should* and ask *Should we go now?* or *Should I sit here?*

Another use is in legal documents or formal rules. A contract to rent an apartment might say *The tenant shall pay the monthly rent by the fifth day of each month.* We also might see a formal rule such as *You shall not leave the building without permission.*

Shall is used mostly with *I* or *we*. In English, we do not say **she shall* or **they shall*. However, when used with contracts or rules, *you shall* may occur.

In traditional grammar books, both *will* and *shall* are used for future tense, but in modern English, *shall* is not frequently used in this way. Today, *shall* mostly occurs either in a question (making a suggestion or asking advice) or in a legal document or rules.

◆ **Question 98** *become* vs. *get*

The word *get* has many meanings, and one of them is "to become." I can say *My job is becoming difficult* or *My job is getting difficult.* Why can't I say *It's getting summer?*

Get has many meanings, and one of the possible meanings is "become." You can say *In December, it becomes dark around 6 PM* or *In December, it gets dark around 6 PM.* Thus, *become* and *get* appear to be interchangeable.

Here are other examples where you can interchange *become* and *get*:

become tired → get tired	become angry → get angry
become sad → get sad	become happy → get happy
become fat → get fat	become red → get red
become quiet → get quiet	become rich → get rich
become lost → get lost	become sick → get sick

All ten of these examples use adjectives such as *hot, tired,* or *rich*. When the word that follows *become* is an adjective, it is usually possible to substitute *get* without any problem.

However, a noun can also follow *become*, so you can say *She became a teacher* or *A caterpillar becomes a butterfly*. When *become* is followed by a noun, we cannot use *get* in its place, so *It's becoming summer* is not possible.

	+ adjective	+ noun
become	We <u>became</u> tired.	A caterpillar becomes a butterfly.
get	We <u>got</u> tired.	*A caterpillar gets a butterfly. This sentence is possible, but the meaning of *get* is different. In this case, it would probably mean "takes" or even "eats," so the sentence is grammatical but does not mean "A caterpillar becomes a butterfly."

◆ **Question 99** *hundred* vs. *hundreds (of)*

Six hundred people attended the meeting. Why do you say *hundred,* not *hundreds*? The number six means it's plural.

When the word *hundred* is preceded by a number, it is always singular: *one hundred, two hundred, three hundred,* etc. We can say *six books,* but we do not say **six hundreds.* In English, the word *hundreds* exists, but there is never a number directly in front of it because *hundreds* means we do not know the number of hundreds.

> *Six <u>hundred</u> people attended the meeting.*

> *<u>Hundreds</u> of people attended the meeting.*

The same rule applies for any kind of counting word such as *dozen, hundred, thousand, million, billion, trillion.*

Counting Word	Counting Word + *–s*
The car costs nine <u>thousand</u> dollars.	She paid <u>thousands</u> of dollars for her car.
She brought eight <u>dozen</u> cookies to school.	She brought <u>dozens</u> of cookies to school.

The counting word ending in *–s* but without a clear number is usually followed by the word *of: two dozen pens* but *dozens of pens.*

A common error is including the word *of* after the counting word when a clear number is present: **two dozen of pens* or **two dozens of pens.*

◆ **Question 100 North American and British English**

What are some differences between North American English grammar and British English grammar? Which English is better? North American English or British English? Is one kind easier than the other?

While this question asks about grammar, the most obvious differences between the two that students might notice are often in vocabulary, pronunciation, spelling, and punctuation.

Differences between North American and British English		
Type	**North American**	**British**
vocabulary	1. apartment 2. vacation 3. French fries	1. flat 2. holiday 3. chips
pronunciation	1. the letter *t* inside a word is not aspirated (*water*); ESL students say it sounds like /d/ 2. the letter *r* is usually sounded after vowels (*father*)	1. the letter *t* inside a word is aspirated (*water*) and is therefore heard more clearly by ESL learners 2. the letter *r* is silent after vowels (*father* sounds like *fath-ah*)
spelling	1. *traveled* with one *l* 2. verbs with *–ize* (*organize*) 3. past tenses with *–ed* instead of *–t* (*dreamed, learned*)	1. *travelled* with double *l* 2. verbs with *–ise* (*organise*) 3. past tenses with *–t* instead of *–ed* (*dreamt, learnt*)
punctuation	1. period after titles (*Mr.*) 2. comma before *and* with 3 items in a series (*red, white, and blue*)	1. no period after titles (*Mr*) 2. no comma before *and* with 3 items in a series (*red, white and blue*)

Some people may believe there are many grammatical differences between North American and British English and that these differences always result in misunderstanding or confusion. However, that is simply not true. Yes, there are some differences but not nearly as many as people will believe.

Grammar Differences between British and North American English	
shall/will for future actions: British English allows both *shall* and *will*. North American English prefers *will*.	Br: We shall arrive in the morning. NA: We will arrive in the morning.
present perfect tense: British English uses this tense more, especially with *already* and *yet*. North American English allows simple past tense.	Br: I've already done that. NA: I already did that. (However, present perfect is also possible.)
prepositions There are some differences with prepositions, especially *at, in,* and *on.*	Br: I watched TV at the weekend. NA: I watched TV on the weekend.
articles There are a few times where North American English uses an article but British English does not.	Br: Sue is in hospital NA: Sue is in the hospital.
subject-verb agreement Collective nouns are viewed as singular in North American English but plural in British English.	Br: The team are winning! NA: The team is winning!

The bottom line here is that grammar of British English is generally not so different from the grammar of American English. To be certain, there are grammar differences, but these are not so important for students learning English as a foreign language. There are many more similarities than differences.

♦♦♦ APPENDIX
Parts of Speech:
Quick Reference Chart

Part of Speech	Definition	Slot	Possible Types	Some Potential ESL Mistakes
Noun	the name of a person, place, thing, idea, quality	• a/an _____ • my _____ • this _____ • 5 _____ s	Common / Proper Concrete / Abstract Count / Non-count	• Plural (*2 childs*) • Suffix (*enjoyation*) • Capitalization (*rome*)
Verb	an action or state of being	• Every day we _____ • That soup _____ delicious • I _____ help you	*be* Regular / Irregular Helping (Auxiliary) Linking Transitive / Intransitive	• No ending for third-person singular (*it rain a lot*) • Tense (*I am here in 2014*) • Negative (*I no work*)
Adjective	describes a noun or a pronoun	• a _____ car • the building is _____ • today's weather is _____	Articles Determiners Quantity Descriptive Demonstrative Possessive	• Position (*a car blue*) • Comparative (*more tall*) • Number (*3 goods boys*)
Adverb	modifies or describes a verb, adjectives, or another adverb	• You sing very _____ • I am _____ tired • She ran _____ quickly	Manner Frequency Degree Frequency	• No ending (*Drive careful!*) • Misplacement (*I go always there*) • No variety (*very…, very…, very…*)

Part of Speech	Definition	Slot	Possible Types	Some Potential ESL Mistakes
Preposition	shows a relationship between a noun (or pronoun) and the rest of the sentence	• _____ the **box** • _____ the **radio** • **I'm interested** _____ **baseball.** • **She's used** _____ **hard work.**	Location Time Lexical/ Grammatical	• Wrong preposition (*on January*) • No preposition (*I looked it*) • Unnecessary preposition (*We enjoyed for it.*)
Conjunction	joins independent clauses; connects words and phrases	• **peanut butter** _____ **jelly** • **Trick** _____ **treat!** • **It was cold,** _____ **we didn't go out.**	Coordinating Subordinating Correlative Conjunctive Adverbs	• Omission (*I study, I work*) • Overuse (*And then… And then…*) • Wrong conjunction
Pronoun	replaces a noun	• **Joe is Thai.** _____ **lives in Bangkok.** • **Pam loves Tim. She loves** _____ **very much.** • **This is the book** _____ **I like.** • **Bo is a cat** _____ **never runs fast.**	Possessive Subject Object Relative Demonstrative Indefinite Reflexive	• Omission (*Is good.*) • Double object (*He is the teacher that I like him.*) • Confusion of he/she (*My mother is here. He is nice.*)

✦✦✦ Answers to Quiz: How Much Grammar Do You Already Know?

1. for begin → to begin

   Question 29: The correct form to express a purpose is an infinitive (*to begin*).

2a. My sister and me → My sister and I

   Question 46: *I* is for subjects; *me* is for objects of a verb or preposition.

2b. the jewelry → jewelry

   Question 8: To talk about a whole category (*jewelry*) in general, English uses no article.

3a. want study → want to study

   Question 29: The verb *want* cannot be followed by a base form of the verb.

3b. the most smart → the smartest

   Question 3: The superlative form of a one-syllable adjective (*smart*) does not add *most*. Instead, it ends in –*est*.

4. good job → a good job

   Question 6: A singular count noun (*job*) needs an article or similar before.

5a. the Disney World → Disney World

   Question 14: Parks usually do not use the definite article (*the*).

5b. gone to there → gone there

   Question 40: The words *here* and *there* do not use *to* with verbs of motion.

6a. I from → I am from

   Question 68: Every sentence must have a verb.

6b. the Kuwait City → Kuwait City

   Question 14: English does not usually allow the definite article (*the*) before the name of a city.

7. It is really good taste → it tastes really good OR it has a really good taste

   Question 83: Soup is not a taste; soup has a taste.

   Question 6: A singular count noun (*taste*) needs an article or similar before.

154

8a. our teacher always give → our teacher always gives

> Question 53: A singular subject (*teacher*) requires a
> singular verb (*gives*).

8b. a homework → homework

> Question 6: The indefinite article (*a*), which means "one,"
> cannot be precede a non-count noun (*homework*).

9. United States → the United States

> Question 10: A country that ends in –s usually needs the
> definite article *the.*

10a. a child young → a young child

> Question 2: An adjective (*young*) precedes a noun (*child*) it
> describes.

10b. interesting → interested

> Question 4: Adjectives that end in –ed (*interested*) are usually
> used to describe people, while adjectives that end in –ing
> (*interesting*) are usually used to describe situations or things.

11a. teacher → a teacher

> Question 7: A singular count noun (*teacher*) needs an
> article or similar word before.

11b. elementary school → an elementary school

> Questions 6 and 7: A singular count noun (*school*) needs an
> article or similar word before. English requires *an* (instead
> of *a*) before the word *elementary* because it begins with a
> vowel sound.

12. can talking → can talk

> Question 76: After a modal (*can*), the base form of the verb
> (*talk*) is required.

13. on August → in August

> Question 35: English uses *in* before months and *on* before
> days.

14. live → have lived

> Question 72: The present perfect (*have lived*) is required
> for actions or situations that began in the past and
> continue until now.

15a. play → playing

> Question 27: The noun form of a verb is a gerund
> (*playing*).

15b. the soccer → soccer

> Question 7: English does not use *the* with names of sports.

16. have → am

Question 83: English uses a form of *be* (not *have*) for age.

17. the traffic problems → traffic problems

Question 8: To talk about a topic in general, English uses the plural form of a noun (*problems*) without the definite article (*the*).

18. of go → of going

Question 27: A gerund (*going*) is required after a preposition (*of*).

19. is → are

Question 53: A plural noun (*activities*) requires a plural verb (*are*).

20a. like eat → like to eat

Question 29: The verb *like* cannot be followed by a base form of the verb.

20b. a lot different kinds → a lot of different kinds

Question 85: *A lot of* is used before nouns (*kinds*); the preposition *of* is necessary.

21. hope have → hope to have

Question 29: The verb *hope* cannot be followed by a base form of the verb.

22a. baseball but → baseball, but

Question 25: A comma is needed between two independent clauses connected by the conjunction *but*.

22b. others sports → other sports (OR another sport)

Question 88: An adjective cannot be plural, so *others* is not possible before the noun *sports*. It can be changed to *other* before a plural noun (*sports*) or *another* before a singular noun (*sport*).

23a. begining → beginning

Question 64: The final *n* in *begin* must be doubled because *begin* ends in consonant-vowel-consonant and the stress is on the second syllable.

23b. spell them correctly → spell correctly

Question 19: Adjective clauses cannot have direct object pronouns (*them*) that refer to the main noun that the clause is describing.

24a. my sister love → my sister loves

>Question 53: A singular noun (*sister*) requires a singular verb (*loves*).

24b. advices → advice

>Question 59: A non-count noun (*advice*) has no plural form.

25. Is → It is (OR It's)

>Question 43: Every verb needs a subject (except in a command).

26. no → not

>Question 69: The correct word to negate a verb is *not*.

27. have been → was

>Question 72: The present perfect (*have been*) cannot be used with a definite past time adverb (*last summer*). Instead, the simple past tense (*was*) is required.

28. grow → grew

>Question 67: The past tense of *grow* (*grew*) is required for a completed situation.

29a. could visit → visited

>Question 77: The modal *could* is not used in the affirmative for a single past action; instead, we use a form of *be able to* (*was able to visit*) or the simple past tense (*visited*).

29b. country → countries

>Question 85: English requires a plural noun (*countries*) after the word *many*.

30. a English teacher → an English teacher

>Question 7: It is necessary to use *an* (instead of *a*) before the word *English* because it begins with a vowel sound.

✦✦✦ Glossary of Grammar Terms

abstract noun: a noun that names an emotion, idea, or quality; an abstract noun cannot be perceived with any of the five senses (*honesty*) (see also concrete noun)

action verbs: verbs that express an action, with or without movement (*cook, eat, help, listen, pour, run, wish*). (see also stative verbs)

active voice: verb form used when the subject is acting upon an object— that is, the receiver of the action (*Mary <u>wrote</u> the letter.*) (see also passive voice)

adjective: a word that describes or limits a noun or pronoun

adjective clause: a dependent clause that functions as an adjective

adverb: a word that modifies a verb, an adjective, or another adverb

adverb clause: a dependent clause that functions as an adverb

affix: a prefix or a suffix

article: an adjective that makes a noun definite or indefinite

aspect: the status of an action—that is, whether it is ongoing or completed (four aspects are simple, progressive, perfect, and perfect progressive)

automaticity: the ability to comprehend or produce language quickly and without explicit effort or attention

auxiliary verb: a helping verb (see also *to be; have, has, had; do, does, did;* modals)

base form of a verb: a verb form without *to* or any endings (also called simple form or dictionary form)

to be: a main verb in English that indicates existence or describes the subject and an auxiliary verb that forms the progressive tenses and the passive voice; the most irregular verb in English with eight forms (*be, am, is, are, was, were, being, been*)

***by* + agent:** phrase used in passive voice constructions to indicate who performed the action (*The house was built <u>by my two uncles</u>.*)

CALP: cognitive academic language proficiency; term applied to the language that an ESL learner needs in order to do well in school—that is, the language of textbooks, academic lectures, and academic papers; CALP takes five to seven (or more) years to develop; contrast with BICS

causative verbs: a verb that expresses the idea of somebody causing something to occur (*get, have, let, make: She <u>had</u> the man change the tire.*)

158

clause: a group of words with both a subject and a verb

cognate: a word in one language that looks or sounds like a word in another language; cognates share a common origin

collective noun: a noun referring to a group of people, things, or animals as a single concept (*jury, government, team, herd*)

common noun: the name of any person, place, or thing (see proper noun)

comparative: adjective or adverb form used for comparing two or more people, things, or actions; formed with *more* (*more quickly*) or *–er* (*taller*)

concrete noun: a noun that you can perceive with your five senses (*newspaper*) (see abstract noun)

conditional sentence: a sentence with a hypothetical situation and its consequence or result

conjugate: to change a verb according to number (singular or plural), person (*I, she*), or tense (present, past)

conjunction: a word that connects parts of a sentence together, including words, phrases, and clauses

conjunctive adverb: transitional devices between two main ideas; the adverb appears with the second of the two ideas (*consequently, however, therefore*)

connectors: a word that connects clauses, phrases, sentences, or other words

consonant-vowel-consonant: See C-V-C.

contraction: a reduced form of a noun or pronoun and a verb (*it's*) made by substituting an apostrophe for the missing letters

coordinating conjunction: a word that connects two independent clauses in a compound sentence (*and, but, or*)

C-V-C: a word ending in consonant-vowel-consonant may double the last consonant (e.g., *stop → stopping*)

corpus: a large collection of spoken or written text that is used for linguistic analysis, such as identifying the most frequent verbs in high school science textbooks

Corpus of Contemporary American English (COCA): the largest searchable and freely available corpus of American English

correlative conjunctions: pairs of words that connect equivalent sentence parts (*both . . . and, neither . . . nor, not only . . . but also*)

count nouns: nouns that can be counted and therefore have both a singular and a plural form (*one book, two books; a child, many children; a fish, five fish*) (see also non-count nouns)

definite article: article that indicates a specific noun (*the*)

demonstrative adjective: an adjective that points out a specific noun (*these books*)

demonstrative pronoun: a pronoun that substitutes for a specific noun that can be understood from context (*those books are mine, but these are yours*)

dependent clause: a clause that cannot stand alone as a complete sentence
descriptive adjective: an adjective that describes a noun, especially its appearance, shape, size, smell, taste, or texture
descriptive grammar: a view of grammar that considers actual usage of language rather than relying on prescribed rules
determiner: a word that precedes a noun and identifies that noun (*a, an, the, this, that, these, those, my, you, his, here, our, their, a few, a little, many, most, one, two,* etc.)
direct object: a noun or pronoun that receives the action of the verb
direct speech: expressing thc message by quoting directly (contrast with **reported speech)**
double negative: the incorrect use of two negative structures within one clause
dummy subject: a word such as *it* that occupies the subject slot but has no clear meaning

–ed participial adjective: a participial adjective ending in *–ed, –en, –ne,* or other irregular form that implies that the noun in question is receiving or being affected by the action (*an amazed viewer*)
EFL: English as a Foreign Language; English learning setting in which English is not spoken widely outside the classroom, such as Japan (see also ESL)
embedded question: a question in the form of a noun clause that is embedded in an independent clause (*No one knows where she lives.*)
ESL: English as a Second Language; English learning setting in which English is widely spoken outside the classroom, such as the U.S., Canada, the U.K., Australia, New Zealand (see also EFL)

fragment: an incomplete sentence frequently consisting of a phrase or a dependent clause that is not properly connected to the main clause

gerund: an *–ing* form that functions as a noun

honorific: a prefix, suffix, or word that indicates the relative social status of the people in a conversation
hypercorrection: a use of incorrect grammar, often where the person is trying to sound correct (*This gift is from my cousin and I,* where people mistakenly believe *I* sounds better than *me*)

idiom: a multi-word expression in which the meanings of the individual words do not equal the meaning of the complete expression (*The test was a piece of cake.*)
imperative sentence: a sentence that expresses a request or a command

indefinite article: articles that do not indicate a specific noun (*a, an*)

indefinite pronoun: pronouns that do not refer to any specific person or thing (*anyone, something*)

independent clause: a clause that can stand alone as a complete sentence

indirect object: an object (person or thing) for whom or to whom or for which or to which something is done; an indirect object occurs before a direct object

infinitive: *to* plus base form a verb (*to go, to be, to take*)

–ing participial adjective: a participial adjective ending in *–ing* that implies that the noun in question is actually doing or causing the action (*an amazing movie*)

intensifier: an adverb such as *very, really,* or *too* that adds emphasis or strength

interference: the application of knowledge of one language into a second language, such as when a Spanish speaker says *I have hungry* in English because Spanish uses *have* instead of *be* in this expression

interjection: a word that expresses strong feeling or emotion

International Phonetic Alphabet (IPA): a system consisting of more than 100 letters and 52 special marks that is used by dictionary writers, linguists, language teachers, foreign language students, singers, and speech pathologists to label the sounds of world languages

intransitive verb: a verb that is never followed by a direct object (*happen*)

irregular verb: a verb whose past tense and past participle forms are not formed by adding *–d* or *–ed*

K–12: term applied to regular subjects taught from kindergarten to twelfth grades in U.S. and Canadian schools

linking verb: a verb that connects the subject and a complement (*be, seem, look*)

long vowel: one of the five vowel sounds whose sound is also the name of the letter: *may, see, light, know, cute*

main clause: the central independent clause of a sentence

modals: an auxiliary verb that expresses feelings, attitudes, or opinions in a verb phrase (*can, might, should*)

modify: describe or limit; often used in discussing the role of adverbs

negative: the "no" form of an utterance; negative grammatical words include *no, not, never, hardly,* and *rarely*

non-action verbs: (see stative verbs)

non-count nouns: nouns that cannot be counted and therefore have only one form (*air, equipment, homework*)

non-separable: term used to describe a phrasal verb in which an object cannot separate the verb and its particle (*takes after her aunt,* **takes her aunt after*)

noun: the name of a person, place, thing, or quality

noun clause: a dependent clause that functions as a noun

null article: the absence of any article before a noun

number: singular or plural in reference to a noun or pronoun

object of preposition: a noun or pronoun after a preposition

object pronoun: a pronoun form that can function as a direct object, indirect object, or object of a preposition (*me, him, her*) (see also subject pronoun)

order of adjectives: sequence of adjectives deemed grammatical in current English usage, namely articles, opinion, size, shape, condition, age, color, and origin (*a magnificent, small, oval, shiny, antique, silver, French spoon*)

participle: a verb form ending in *–ing, –ed* or *–en* that functions as an adjective or part of a verb

particle: second part of a phrasal verb

part of speech: one of the traditional eight categories of words, including noun, pronoun, adjective, adverb, verb, preposition, conjunction, interjection

passive voice: verb form used when the subject is being acted upon an object—that is, the agent of the action (*The letter was written by Mary.*) (see also active voice)

past participle: a participle formed with *–d* or *–ed* for regular verbs and with *–en, –ne,* or other ways for irregular verbs that is used in the perfect tenses, passive voice, or as an adjective

perfect modal: a verb structure consisting of a modal + a form of *have* + past participle (*should have known, might have gone*)

perfect tenses: present perfect tense, present perfect progressive tense, past perfect tense, past perfect progressive tense, future perfect tense, future perfect progressive tense; verb tenses consisting of a form of the auxiliary verb *have* and a past participle

phrasal modal: a modal that has more than one word; examples include *be able to, would rather, had better*

phrasal verb: a verb and its particle (or preposition) (*take after, look over, call off*)

phrase: a group of words that functions as a single part of speech

plural: the form that represents more than one person, place, or thing

polysemous: having multiple meanings

possessive adjective: an adjective that indicates ownership (*my, your, our*)

possessive pronoun: a pronoun that takes the place of a possessive word and its object (*mine, yours, ours*)

preposition: a word that shows the relationship between a noun (or pronoun) and the rest of the sentence

prepositional phrase: combination of a preposition and its object (and any modifiers or describing words)

prescriptive grammar: a view of grammar that prescribes, or dictates, exactly what we should or should not say without any consideration of actual usage

present participle: a participle formed with *–ing* that is used in the progressive tenses or as an adjective

principal parts of a verb: the four forms of a verb from which all tenses of the verb can be made—namely base form, past tense, past participle, present participle (*go, went, gone, going*); some sources do not count the present participle as a principal part of a verb.

progressive tenses: present progressive tense, present perfect progressive tense, past progressive tense, past perfect progressive tense, future progressive tense, future perfect progressive tense; verb tenses that contain a form of the verb *to be* and a present participle

pronoun: a word that can take the place of a noun

proper noun: the name of a specific person, place, or thing (see also common noun)

quantifiers: numbers and words such as *many, much, a few, a little* that function as adjectives (also called quantity adjectives)

reciprocal pronoun: a pronoun that denotes that two or more people did an action and received the benefit of that action (*My aunt and my mom often call each other*)

reflexive pronoun: a pronoun ending in *–self* that is preceded by the noun or pronoun to which it refers inside the same clause

register: the level of formality of language

regular verb: a verb whose past tense and past participle forms end in *–d or –ed*

relative clause: an adjective clause

relative pronoun: a pronoun that connects a relative clause to the rest of the sentence (*who, that, which, whom*)

reported speech: expressing the message without quoting (as is done in **direct speech**)

reporting verbs: verbs such as *say, tell,* and *recommend* that report, either through a direct quote or paraphrase, what someone has said

schwa /ə/: vowel sound that occurs in unstressed syllables (so<u>f</u>a, lem<u>o</u>n, grad<u>e</u>d)

semantics: the meaning of a word or sentence

separable: term used to describe a phrasal verb in which an object can separate the verb and its particle (*pick up the papers, pick the papers up*)

short vowel: one of the five vowel sounds in these words: *cat, pet, sit, not, but*

simple form of a verb: see base form of a verb

simple sentence: a sentence consisting of one independent clause (i.e., one subject-verb relationship)

singular: the form that represents one person, place, or thing

stative verbs: verbs that express state, desire, opinion, or possession (*appear, be, believe, feel, like, need, own, possess, prefer, seem, smell, sound, taste, want*) (see also action verbs)

stress: the emphasis given to a certain syllable in a word (PRE-sent *vs.* pre-SENT)

subject: part of a sentence excluding the predicate; the noun (or pronoun) and anything that modifies it that performs the action of the verb (*Where is <u>she</u>? Rarely is <u>she</u> late.*)

subject pronoun: a pronoun that can function as the subject of a sentence (*I, he, she*) (see also object pronoun)

subject-verb agreement: condition in which the subject and the verb agree in number—that is, singular subjects accompany singular verbs and plural subjects accompany plural verbs

subjunctive: the mood of a verb that shows hopes, doubts, or wishes (*I recommend that you <u>be</u> given this job.*)

subordinate clause: a dependent clause

subordinating conjunction: a word that introduces an adverb clause and explains its relationship to the main part of the sentence (*after, because, while*)

suffix: a word ending that changes the meaning of the word (*sad, sadder*) or its part of speech (*sad, sadness*)

superlative: the highest level of an adjective or adverb; formed with *the most* (*the most quickly*) or *–est* (*the tallest*)

syntax: the rules that show how the words of a language can be arranged to make a phrase or sentence

third person: subject pronouns *he, she, it* (singular) and *they* (plural)

transitive verb: a verb that requires a direct object (*put*)

verb: a word that shows action or state of being

verb phrase: the main verb plus any auxiliary verbs; the complete verb in the predicate; a verb phrase can vary from one verb (*She <u>drove</u> the car to the beach*) to five verbs (*The car <u>should have been being driven</u> more slowly*)

verb tense: simply put, the time of the action or state conveyed by the verb

voiced sounds: sounds produced by moving or vibrating the vocal cords (/b/, /g/, /v/)

voiceless sounds: sounds produced without moving or vibrating the vocal cords (/p/, /k/, /f/)

***wh-* question:** an information question that begins with a *wh-* word such as *who, what,* or *where* (compare with yes-no question)

word part: a prefix, a root (base), or a suffix of a word

word wall: an organized and often interactive display of words or other information on a wall or bulletin board that allows visual reference to foster recycling and mastery

yes-no question: an information question for which the answer is either *yes* or *no*

◆◆◆ REFERENCES

Alzuhairy, U. (2016). *A corpus analysis of the distribution of verb tenses in college writing* (Master's thesis). University of Central Florida, Orlando.

Biber, D., Johansson, S., Leech, G., Conrad, S., and Finegan, E. (1999). *Longman grammar of spoken and written English*. New York: Pearson.

Davies, M. (2008–). *The corpus of contemporary American English (COCA): 560 million words, 1990–present. Available online at http://corpus.byu.edu/coca*

Folse, K. (2004). *Vocabulary myths: Applying second language research to classroom teaching*. Ann Arbor: University of Michigan Press.

Folse, K. (2016). *Keys to teaching grammar to English language learners: A practical handbook* (2nd ed.). Ann Arbor: University of Michigan Press.

Qahtani, B. (2017). *The frequency of the twelve verb tenses in history papers written by university native writers*. (Master's thesis). University of Central Florida, Orlando.

Reilly, N. (2013). *A comparative analysis of present and past participal adjectives and their collocations in the Corpus of Contemporary American English (COCA)*. (Master's thesis). University of Central Florida, Orlando.

Swan, M., & Smith, B. (Eds.). (2001). *Learner English: A teacher's guide to interference and other problems* (2nd ed.). Cambridge: Cambridge University Press.

West, M. (1953). *A general service list of English words*. London: Longman, Green & Co.

✦✦✦ INDEX

167